JCL for IBM VSE Systems

Related Books from the Wiley Press

ANS COBOL, 2nd ed., Ashley
COBOL for Microcomputers, Ashley and Fernandez
Structured COBOL, Ashley
The Complete FORTH, Winfield
Fortran IV, 2nd ed., Friedmann, Greenberg and Hoffberg
PC DOS, 2nd ed., Ashley and Fernandez
Introduction to Data Processing, 3rd ed., Harris
Learning FORTH, Armstrong

JCL for
IBM VSE Systems

Ruth Ashley
Judi Fernandez
Sharon Beamesderfer

A WILEY PRESS BOOK
John Wiley & Sons, Inc.
New York • Chichester • Brisbane • Toronto • Singapore

Our thanks to Jeff Stillwell for his many helpful technical comments and to Edith Messenger for her patience and accuracy in typing this manuscript with all its JCL code.

Publisher: Stephen Kippur
Editor: Theron Shreve
Managing Editor: Katherine Schowalter
Design, Composition & Make-Up: Ganis & Harris, Inc.

Library of Congress Cataloging-in-Publication Data

Ashley, Ruth.
    JCL for IBM VSE systems.

    1. IBM VSE (Computer operating system) 2. Job Control Language (Computer program language)
I. Fernandez, Judi N., 1941-   . II. Beamesderfer, Sharon. III. Title.
QA76.76.063A84   1986   005.4'3   85-20313
ISBN 0-471-82298-1

Printed in the United States of America

86 87 10 9 8 7 6 5 4 3 2 1

Contents

Preface

IBM offers several operating systems for its mainframes, including the Disk Operating System/Virtual Storage Extended (DOS/VSE), which we usually call simply VSE. Thousands of IBM mainframe installations use VSE, including most of the 4300 series of computers. Their operators, programmers, and end users must communicate with and control the system through VSE's Job Control Language (JCL).

It's surprising how many people who work with VSE every day do not understand JCL—are even afraid of it. To get their processing work done, they borrow other people's JCL without really understanding it or they let the system editor generate their JCL for them. They have no idea of the full extent of the system's capabilities and how to make all that power work for them.

JCL is not hard to understand. It's a computer language, pretty much like other computer languages. It has a vocabulary of operations and parameters related directly to VSE's features. It has a syntax (admittedly an awkward, unfriendly syntax). As with most languages, it's difficult to learn JCL by reading a reference manual, just as it's difficult to learn English by reading a dictionary.

This book is a Self-Teaching Guide, not a reference manual. It presents JCL from a functional standpoint, not in alphabetical order. That is, it looks at functions that users want to accomplish and explains the proper code to accomplish them. It starts with simple tasks, such as running a program with unit record I/O, and builds step-by-step toward more complicated tasks: using tape and disk files, using private libraries, overriding cataloged procedures, and so forth. Every new concept is illustrated with diagrams, job-relevant examples, and exercises to let you practice and learn, with correct answers immediately following each exercise. Be sure to work the exercises, writing out all your answers. These exercises are the key to successfully learning JCL.

This is an introductory book. It assumes you know nothing about JCL, at the start. It presents JCL's most commonly used features, things you'll use every day. It does not get into less-used facilities, although the final chapter briefly describes some of these so you'll know they exist.

This book speaks directly to programmers at VSE installations, showing them how to compile (or assemble), link edit, test, and catalog programs; how to create, catalog, and use cataloged procedures; how to use private libraries; and so forth. However, nonprogramming readers will also find much useful information here, especially in the earlier chapters that deal with the execution of existing programs.

One final word: Few installations use pure "vanilla" JCL. Your installation may have added system features that give you more power, but that also change the JCL code slightly. Furthermore, your installation may have set JCL usage standards you'll need to adhere to. So, as you read this book, keep checking with your local experts to find out how things are done at your installation.

chapter one

Before We Begin

Job Control Language (JCL) is used to control the DOS/VSE operating system. But what is DOS/VSE? For that matter, what's an operating system? This chapter will tell you. It introduces some basic concepts and terminology you will use throughout this book and on the job. When you have completed this chapter, you'll be able to:

✔ Identify descriptions of an operating system

✔ Identify important DOS/VSE programs

✔ Identify the main purpose of Job Control Language

✔ Identify the DOS/VSE libraries

✔ Identify descriptions of virtual storage and multiprogramming

What Is an Operating System?

An *operating system* is a group of system programs that control the computer's resources (memory, storage, CPU time, etc.) so that people can use the computer efficiently. The operating system must maximize *throughput* (that is, the number of programs that are processed in a given period of time), minimize down time, minimize human intervention, avoid system crashes, and protect each user's programs and data.

Operating systems are like ticket takers in amusement parks. Ticket takers do a lot more than just receive tickets as people file past. They control the waiting line, making sure people wait their turn and don't endanger others with unsafe behavior. When the ride is ready, they admit riders in turn and fill as many seats as possible. Sometimes, they might take people out of order in the line to fill empty seats. They refuse to admit unqualified riders (such as children too short for a rough ride). They check the safety precautions before starting the ride. During the ride, they might monitor the behavior of the riders for safety. And they might even control the ride time based on the length of the waiting line. For these reasons, we can say they are controlling the resources of the ride.

Now let's look at how a large-scale operating system such as DOS/VSE controls the computer's resources. It handles all processing requests, forming waiting lines called *queues* like the ones at the amusement park; it maintains control of the queues. When the computer is available, the operating system pulls the next job from the appropriate queue, loads the program, locates the files, and starts the program. If anything is wrong with the job, such as requesting too much memory or a nonexistent file, it rejects the job. A sophisticated operating system such as DOS/VSE can run several programs concurrently, letting each program in turn have control of the computer for short periods of time (multiprogramming).

The operating system also manages the computer while programs are running. It maintains ultimate control over memory usage, providing memory space for each program that is executing and preventing one program from encroaching on another's memory space. The operating system maintains control over all storage facilities such as disk and tape; it decides which

Figure 1.1 DOS/VSE Controls the Use of the Computer

program can use which device and handles all I/O requests. No application program actually reads and writes on any device. The application program requests an I/O service; the operating system does the reading and writing.

Why do operating systems do these things? They do these things so that many different users, from many different departments and with many different needs, can all use the same system efficiently and effectively. The operating system minimizes the amount of time it takes to load and start a new program so that the computer is working as much as possible. This helps to maximize throughput; it also means that people's requests get serviced sooner. The operating system protects each user's data and programs from accidental or intentional damage by other programs; this provides security and protects the integrity of data files. Otherwise, no one would want to use the computer.

Most operating systems also offer a wide variety of services that make programming easier: assemblers and compilers so you don't have to code machine language; access method programs so you don't have to create your own file structures and write your own I/O routines (heaven forbid); online editors so you can work at a terminal; and so forth.

To summarize, every computer except a dedicated one needs an operating system. The larger the computer and the more users, the more complex and sophisticated the operating system needs to be. The operating system makes it possible for a variety of people to share the computer without winding up at each other's throats.

What Is DOS/VSE?

DOS/VSE stands for Disk Operating System/Virtual Storage Extended. IBM developed this operating system from an earlier one for use on its System/370, 303X, and 4300 machines, and any machine with an architecture similar to these.

The word "disk" means that all the operating system programs reside on disk. Earlier systems were on tape.

Using disk packs as auxiliary storage also makes possible the concept of *virtual storage*, which we'll explore in some detail later on in this chapter. For now, we can say that programs and data are transferred between memory and disk storage so that only the information immediately required by the executing program is in memory. The effect of virtual storage is that the machine seems to have a far greater internal storage capacity than its physical limits.

✓ Check Your Understanding

1. Which phrase best describes an operating system?
   a. A hardware device
   b. A group of system programs
   c. A team of humans
   d. The CPU

2. What is an operating system's function?
   a. Control the computer's resources
   b. Replace programmers
   c. Eliminate the need for a central computer site
   d. Replace operators

3. The number of programs processed in a given period of time is called:
   a. Input
   b. Output
   c. Throughput

4. A waiting line is also called a:
   a. Batch
   b. Queue
   c. Library

5. Select features of large-scale operating systems such as DOS/VSE.
   a. Maintain control over internal storage (memory)
   b. Maintain control over external storage (disks, etc.)
   c. Supervise job queues
   d. Supervise execution of programs
   e. Offer a variety of programmer services
   f. All of the above

6. What do the letters DOS/VSE stand for?

7. On what type of storage device does DOS/VSE reside?

8. Which statement describes virtual storage?
    a. Disk packs are used to make internal storage appear larger.
    b. The CPU and internal storage are on the same microchip, speeding data transfers.
    c. The different programs executing concurrently each use a different memory device.

✔ Answers

1. b

2. a

3. c

4. b

5. f

6. Disk Operating System/Virtual Storage Extended

7. Disk

8. a

DOS/VSE Programs

DOS/VSE consists of several system programs. Here we'll highlight the ones most important to programmers.

The *Supervisor* is probably the most important program in DOS/VSE because it controls the rest of the operating system. It acts as an interface between your application program and the system resources. Whenever your program requests a system service such as reading a record, control is passed to the

Supervisor, which loads and executes the appropriate system program.

The Supervisor is loaded into main storage at location 000000 each time the system is brought up, and it remains there as long as DOS/VSE is running. The Supervisor calls in other programs as needed to process your job.

The *Initial Program Load* (IPL) program brings up the system each day and loads the Supervisor into its main storage location. We mention this because you'll hear people talking about having to "IPL the system."

Another important DOS/VSE program is the *Job Control Program* (JCP). The JCP is the program responsible for controlling processing requests. When you want to execute a program, you code a request using Job Control Language (JCL). You submit the request from your terminal (or a card reader). The JCP reads your JCL statements and tells the Supervisor which programs to execute and which files to look for.

Notice the role of JCL in this process. You use JCL to communicate with, and control, the JCP. That's what you'll learn to do in this book.

Data management programs handle files. Various types of access method programs are available to process your I/O requests. Data management programs handle label processing, security, reading, writing, and so forth.

Library management programs organize and maintain libraries of information on disk. The libraries are very important to programmers, as all programs are kept in libraries. You'll be learning more about them later in this chapter.

Utility programs perform common, everyday functions such as making backup copies of files, transferring files from one storage medium to another, printing file contents, and so forth. DOS/VSE includes several utility programs.

The *Assembler* program translates a source program written in Assembler Language into machine language. Assembler Language is so close to machine language that it is often used by system programmers as they maintain and enhance the operating system.

The *Linkage Editor* program is used by programmers to combine program modules that have been assembled or compiled separately. This makes modular programming easier.

Programmers can avoid a lot of repetitive coding by saving commonly used routines and *linking* them into their programs. Also, several programmers can work on one project and *link* their modules together at the appropriate time.

Debugging aids assist programmers in locating errors in their source programs. Programmers use many sources of information to track down errors: assembler or compiler listings, linkage editor listings, listings of file labels and contents, and so forth. In addition, DOS/VSE includes two programs to aid debugging:

- A *Trace Facility* produces a listing of routines, instructions, and data as they are being processed. The programmer uses the trace listing to see what the computer did, when.
- A *Dump Facility* prints the contents of the registers and virtual storage. Programmers who can interpret the hexadecimal codes can find out exactly what was in memory at critical times during program execution. This can help in pinning down a tricky logic error.

There are a number of optional programs that may be ordered as part of an operating system, much as you would order options for a new car. Some typical options are compilers for various languages such as COBOL, PL/I, and Fortran, more sophisticated access method programs such as VSAM, and telecommunication support packages such as VTAM and BTAM. Two very important options are ICCF and POWER. ICCF (Interactive Computing and Control Facility) gives you the ability to program at a terminal. With ICCF you can create a source program file, then submit it to be compiled, link edited, and tested. You can see the results at your terminal, make changes in the source file, and try again.

POWER is a unit record management program that helps increase throughput. POWER accepts jobs submitted through ICCF, as well as other ways, queues them, prioritizes them, etc. It also captures unit record output from jobs and queues it until the printer or punch is available. You can examine the POWER queues through ICCF to find out where your job is and estimate how long it will be before it gets processed. You can also pull

output out of a POWER queue and examine it at your terminal.
  Your installation will probably have both these programs, which are so useful to application programmers and others. You should spend some time learning to use them. This book, which covers only JCL, does not show you how.

✓ Check Your Understanding

1. What is the most important program in the operating system? Why is it so important?

2. Which program combines compiled modules to produce an executable program?

3. Programs that perform routine functions such as copying files are called _____ programs.

4. Two DOS/VSE debugging aids are the _____ facility and the _____ facility.

5. Which DOS/VSE program is responsible for handling job requests?

6. What language do you use to submit job requests?

✔ Answers

1. The Supervisor; because it controls the rest of the operating system

2. The Linkage Editor

3. Utility

4. Trace; Dump

5. The Job Control Program (JCP)

6. Job Control Language (JCL)

Virtual Storage

Now that you've seen what DOS/VSE is and what some of its programs are, let's look at a major feature of this operating system: virtual storage.

Main storage is the part of the system containing the programs and data the computer is currently using. It is also known as *memory* or *internal storage.* The larger main storage is, the better for throughput. Also, programming is easier when you don't have to worry about main storage limitations.

Virtual storage is created when the computer's memory is enhanced by disk storage to create an apparent memory space much larger than the physical reality.

Figure 1.2 illustrates virtual storage operation. Every program is divided into small pieces called *pages,* and only those pages most immediately required by the program in progress are kept in main storage. Pages not needed right now are stored temporarily on a disk pack. If the program references an instruction or data item currently stored on the disk pack, the system brings the necessary page into main storage. This process is called *paging.* In this way, the computer operates as though its storage capacity were far greater than the amount of main storage physically available. This large, conceptual area is called *virtual storage.*

Figure 1.2 Virtual Storage

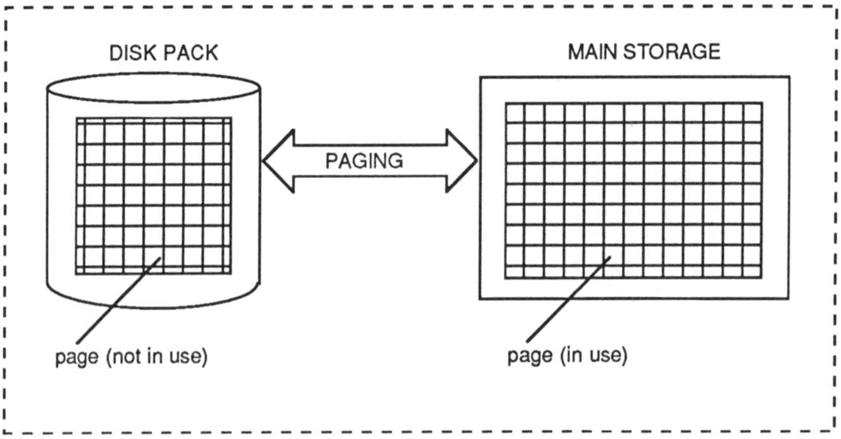

DISK PACK   MAIN STORAGE

PAGING

page (not in use)   page (in use)

As a programmer, you won't really be aware of how the computer uses its virtual storage, and you won't have much control over it. You will, however, see the effects of virtual storage indirectly—nearly unlimited memory and somewhat slower processing when paging takes place. If you've ever had to break up a program because it wouldn't fit into the available memory space, you'll appreciate virtual storage.

✓ Check Your Understanding

1. A conceptual memory area that permits the computer to operate as though its storage capacity were greater than the amount of physical memory is known as _____.

2. The process of transferring pages between main and auxiliary storage is called _____.

3. Which statements are true?
   a. Virtual storage makes programming harder, but the payoff is worth it.
   b. Paging slows program execution.
   c. Virtual storage increases throughput.

✔ Answers

1. Virtual storage

2. Paging

3. b and c

Multiprogramming

Now let's look at another major DOS/VSE feature: running two or more programs concurrently.

DOS/VSE divides virtual storage into several areas called

partitions. (See Figure 1.3.) By processing one program in each partition, several programs may be executed concurrently (during the same time period). This is called *multiprogramming.*

Figure 1.3 Partitions in Virtual Storage

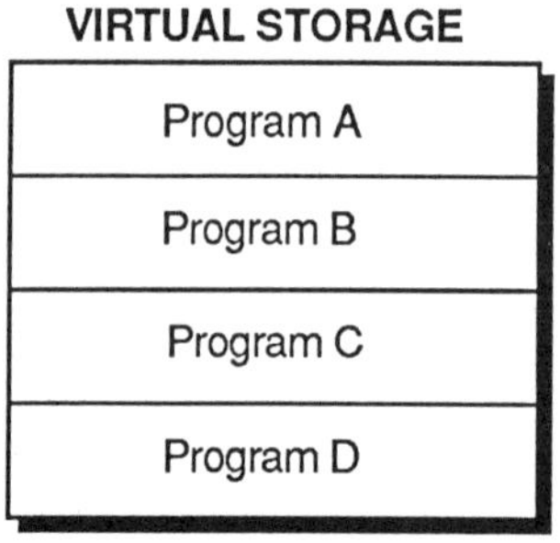

VIRTUAL STORAGE

Program A
Program B
Program C
Program D

The number and size of the partitions are determined by the installation. Our example in Figure 1.3 has its virtual storage divided into four partitions. As you see in the figure, four different programs are running, one in each partition. The CPU switches its attention from one to the other. This is possible because the CPU is not required for I/O operations, which are accomplished by separate processors. Thus, when Program A is waiting for a READ or WRITE operation to be completed, the CPU can focus its attention on another program, say Program C. When Program C must wait for an I/O operation, the CPU switches its attention to yet another program. This all happens in microseconds, so it appears that the programs are executing all at the same time, but really they are taking turns.

Each partition is protected from the other partitions so that pages from one program don't get mixed up with pages from other programs while the CPU's attention is jumping back and forth. The Supervisor maintains control over the partitions and their programs.

Your installation assigns a priority to each partition. A partition with a high priority receives the CPU's attention before a partition having a lower priority. Your installation might have some rules regarding which partitions can be used to run which jobs, and you may be asked to run your jobs in a certain partition and to avoid other partitions. This helps save the higher priority partitions for the jobs that need faster turnaround.

How does multiprogramming affect you? It seems as though your program is executing continuously from start to finish, but in fact it's being interrupted constantly as the CPU is shared by different programs. Technically, each individual program is being executed more slowly than it would be if it had exclusive use of the computer—but the overall processing time for all the programs is faster than it would be if they were done separately because the CPU isn't waiting for I/O operations. So you can run more programs per day than in a single-programming system.

Check Your Understanding

1. Concurrent execution of several programs is known as
   _____.

2. Which operating system program controls multiprogramming?

3. Which statement best describes multiprogramming?
   a. One instruction is executed from Program A, then one from Program B, etc.
   b. Program A is executed until it requests an I/O service, then control goes to Program B, etc.
   c. Each program has a separate CPU and all programs execute simultaneously.

✔ Answers

1. Multiprogramming

2. The Supervisor

3. b

DOS/VSE Libraries

The DOS/VSE libraries have significant impact on the programmer's job. Let's take a closer look at these important DOS/VSE facilities, which are depicted in Figure 1.4.

You might be asking, "What's a library?" Some people define it as a collection of related files, but it's more like one large file

Figure 1.4 The DOS/VSE System Libraries

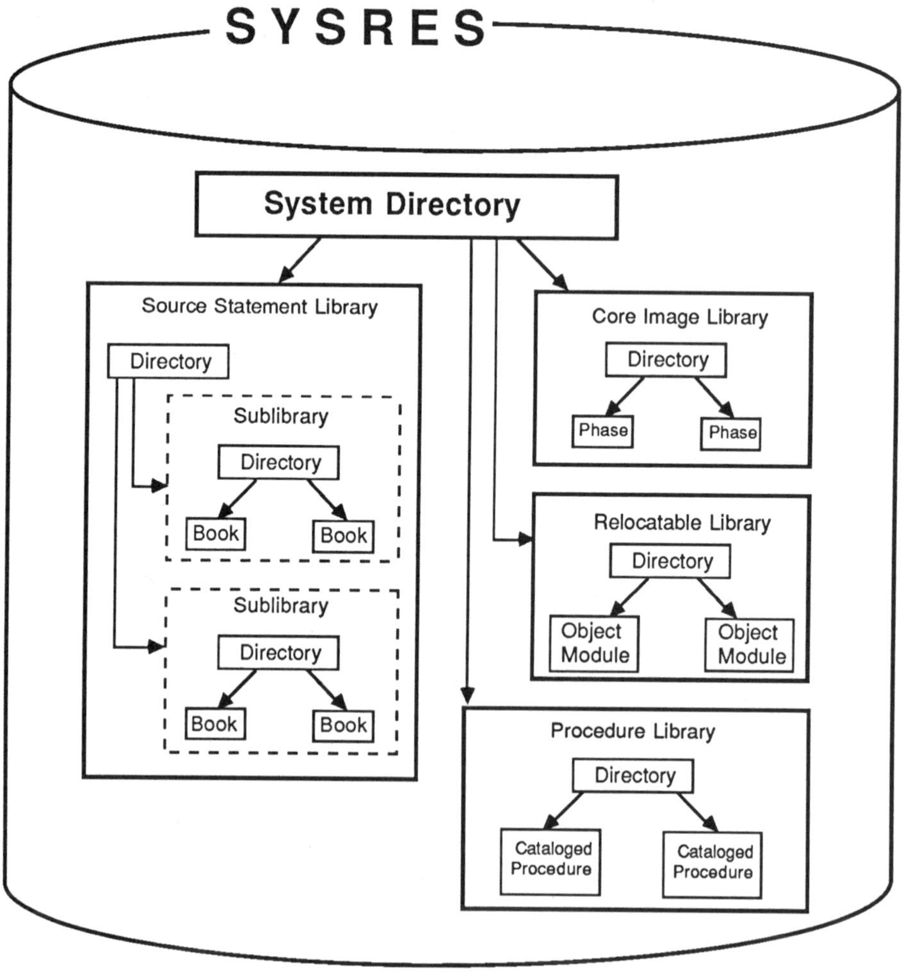

SYSRES

System Directory

Source Statement Library
Directory
Sublibrary
Directory
Book   Book
Sublibrary
Directory
Book   Book

Core Image Library
Directory
Phase   Phase

Relocatable Library
Directory
Object Module   Object Module

Procedure Library
Directory
Cataloged Procedure   Cataloged Procedure

broken into subfiles, each subfile acting like a separate file. For example, all executable programs are kept in a library called the Core Image Library. You can't execute a program under DOS/VSE if it isn't in the Core Image Library. The Core Image Library is one file; each program is like a subfile.

Each library contains a directory of the names of all elements, such as programs, in the library and the disk addresses where they can be found. The directory helps speed access to the individual elements.

Libraries are kept on disk for fast access and easy maintenance. In a normal DOS/VSE installation, the libraries are accessed continually and updated many, many times per day. All the system libraries reside on the same disk, known as the System Residence Pack, or SYSRES. However, your application might also have private libraries not available to other applications at your installation. These private libraries reside on private volumes and may be available only to certain partitions.

One advantage of having private libraries is that programs being written or tested can be kept separate from the production programs residing in the system libraries. Once the programs are ready for operational status, they may be retained in the private library or copied into a system library, depending on the wishes of the user.

Another advantage of having a private Core Image Library is that it helps to reduce the demand for space on SYSRES. Because the system Core Image Library is accessed frequently (several times per minute), keeping it as small as possible permits faster access time (fewer directory entries to search).

DOS/VSE recognizes four types of libraries, discussed in detail below. Your installation may not use all four types, but most installations do.

Source Statement Library

The Source Statement Library contains groups of frequently used source statements. For example, an installation's major file and record definitions are often kept in the Source Statement Library so they can be copied into programs that access the files. The individual elements in the Source Statement Library are called *books*. Books may be copied from the Source Statement Library into source programs during compilation, thus saving the programmer much time and many keystrokes.

As Figure 1.4 shows, the Source Statement Library is divided into several sublibraries to keep various languages and departments separate. This is the only DOS/VSE library with sublibraries. Each sublibrary has a single-character name. IBM has predefined some of the sublibraries:

- A and E are Assembler Language sublibraries
- C is the COBOL sublibrary

IBM reserves the B, D, F, I, P, R, and Z sublibraries for its own use. Your installation uses the remaining sublibraries as it wishes. Take the time to find out what the Source Statement sublibraries are at your installation; you'll need to use them.

The Source Statement Library is accessed by the assembler or by any of the compilers in response to COPY commands in a source program and assembler macros. You'll learn how to access the Source Statement Library later in this book.

Relocatable Library

The Relocatable Library stores standard routines in object code. These routines are called *object modules* and are used frequently in larger programs. These modules have been compiled but not link edited. Examples of object modules are the vendor-supplied routines that handle data transfer to and from the I/O devices.

The Linkage Editor accesses the Relocatable Library at link edit time and combines the object modules with the object code output from the compiler to form the executable program that it places in the Core Image Library.

Core Image Library

This library contains executable programs called *phases*. A phase is created in two steps: a source program is translated into object code by a compiler or assembler, and then the Linkage Editor combines that code with various modules from the Relocatable Library. The Linkage Editor also places the completed phase into the Core Image Library.

A phase doesn't have to be an entire program. It could be just part of a program, but it must be in object code and it must be link edited before arriving in the Core Image Library.

Procedure Library

The Procedure Library stores frequently used sets of Job Control Language statements. Each set of statements is called a *cataloged procedure.*

A typical example of a procedure would be a set of statements designed to compile, link edit, and then execute a program.

Cataloged procedures can save you an enormous amount of time and hassle. Instead of coding and typing a complicated procedure every time you use it, several times a day, you simply call the procedure up from the library. No problem.

Cataloged procedures make life easier for end users, too. When you put a new program into production, you catalog the user's JCL. Then they don't have to code, or even understand, JCL in order to run their program.

Figure 1.5, on the following page, summarizes the contents of the various libraries and shows how you can access them. Don't worry about the "JCL or Program Statement" column. We'll get to that in a later chapter.

How Are the Libraries Maintained?

The operating system contains a group of programs devoted to maintaining libraries. These programs are divided into two types:

- The maintenance program (MAINT), which lets you add, delete, replace, condense, or update the library elements
- A group of six service programs that obtain printed listings of the library elements

You'll be learning to use some of these programs later in this book.

Figure 1.5 Using the DOS/VSE Libraries

Name	Contents	Accessed by	JCL or Program Statement
Source Statement	*Books* in source code (organized in sublibraries)	Compilers and Assembler	`COPY bookname` `bookname` (in Assembler)
Relocatable	*Object modules,* compiled but not link edited	Linkage Editor	`CALL modulename` `INCLUDE modulename`
Core Image	*Phases* in compiled and link edited object code	Job Control Program; Supervisor	`// EXEC phasename`
Procedure	*Cataloged procedures* (Sets of Job Control Language statements)	Job Control Program	`// EXEC PROC=procname`

✓ Check Your Understanding

1. All the operating system programs and system (public) libraries reside on the same disk pack. What is it called?

2. The Source Statement Library contains elements called _____ .

3. The Relocatable Library contains _____ .

4. The Core Image Library contains _____.

5. Use an X to mark whether the contents of each type of library are in source code, object code, or JCL and whether they have been link edited.

Library	Source Code?	Object Code?	JCL?	Link Edited?
a. Source Statement	_____	_____	_____	_____
b. Relocatable	_____	_____	_____	_____
c. Core Image	_____	_____	_____	_____
d. Procedure	_____	_____	_____	_____

✔ **Answers**

1. System Residence (SYSRES)

2. Books

3. Object modules

4. Phases

5. a. Source code
   b. Object code
   c. Object code, link edited
   d. JCL

Chapter Summary

An operating system is a group of programs that control the computer's resources. Major DOS/VSE programs are:

- The Supervisor, which controls the rest of the system
- IPL, which starts up the system
- The JCP, which selects jobs for execution
- Data management programs, which handle files
- The Assembler, which translates Assembler Language programs
- The Linkage Editor, which combines object modules
- Debugging aids, which help debug programs
- Library management programs, which maintain the libraries
- Utility programs, which perform common functions

Job Control Language (JCL) communicates with the JCP. Virtual storage lets the computer use more main storage than really exists. Paging transfers program pages between the virtual storage disk and memory. Multiprogramming is the concurrent processing of several programs.

The libraries are:

- Source Statement, which contains books of code in source language to be copied into source programs
- Relocatable, which contains object-code modules to be linked into executable programs
- Core Image, which contains executable programs called phases
- Procedure, which contains sets of JCL statements

✓ Chapter Exercise

1. Which statements describe an operating system?
   a. A special piece of hardware attached to the computer
   b. Decides which executing program will have control of the CPU
   c. Handles many chores automatically, without human intervention
   d. Has no control over an application program's use of the system resources
   e. Keeps instructions in concurrently executing programs from getting mixed up with each other

2. Which is *not* one of the operating system's main functions?
   a. Managing data
   b. Correcting errors in executing programs
   c. Controlling the computer's resources
   d. Controlling the execution of programs

3. Identify the function of each program. (Some functions are not used.)

   _____ a. Job Control Program
   _____ b. Initial Program Load
   _____ c. Supervisor
   _____ d. Assembler
   _____ e. Data Management
   _____ f. Linkage Editor
   _____ g. Trace Facility
   _____ h. Dump Facility
   _____ i. Utility

   A. Controls the rest of the system
   B. Combines object modules
   C. Performs often used functions
   D. Selects programs for execution
   E. Starts the system
   F. Translates Assembler Language programs
   G. Lists library contents
   H. Lists memory contents
   I. Reads/writes records
   J. Lists routines and their data in order of execution

4. What language do you use to communicate with the JCP?

5. Identify the libraries described below.
    a. Contains portions of programs in source code that you can copy into your source program
    b. Contains executable programs (link edited and ready to go)
    c. Contains object modules that you can link into your programs
    d. Contains sets of JCL statements
    e. Contains phases
    f. Contains cataloged procedures
    g. Contains books
    h. Divided into sublibraries

6. Which statements are true about virtual storage?
    a. The programmer directly controls virtual storage.
    b. Virtual storage apparently provides a greater amount of main storage space than the machine's actual physical capacity.
    c. Virtual storage uses an auxiliary storage medium to hold information not needed immediately by the executing program.
    d. Programs are divided into sections called partitions.
    e. Transferring information between main storage and the backup disk is called paging.

7. Which statements are true about multiprogramming?
    a. Multiprogramming allows several programs to execute concurrently, one per partition.
    b. Multiprogramming means that instructions from several programs are executing at exactly the same moment.
    c. Multiprogramming means that processing is somewhat slower than would be the case if only one program were executing.

8. Ask around and find the answers to these questions about the system where you work:
    a. How many partitions?
    b. How big is each partition?
    c. Which partitions have the highest priority?
    d. The lowest priority?

e. Which partitions can you use for compiling?

f. Testing?

g. Which partitions, if any, are you not allowed to use?

h. Which system libraries are available to you?

i. Which private libraries?

j. Which sublibraries of the Source Statement Library are available to you?

✔ Answers to Chapter Exercise

1. b, c, e

2. b

3. a - D; b - E; c - A; d - F; e - I; f - B; g - J; h - H; i - C

4. Job Control Language (JCL)

5. a. Source Statement Library
   b. Core Image Library
   c. Relocatable Library
   d. Procedure Library
   e. Core Image Library
   f. Procedure Library
   g. Source Statement Library
   h. Source Statement Library

6. b, c, e

7. a, c

8. The answers depend on your installation.

chapter two

Getting Started

Now you're ready to start learning how to code JCL. This chapter looks at the simplest jobs, those that use unit record files ("card" and print) only.

When you have finished this chapter, you will be able to:

✔   Identify correct definitions of "job," "job step," and "job stream"

✔   Code JOB statements

✔   Code EXEC statements

✔   Code delimiter statements

✔   Code comment statements

✔   Code single-step jobs including input unit-record data

✔   Code multistep jobs including input unit-record data

Jobs, Job Steps, and Job Streams

Let's look at a typical data processing job. Suppose Figure 2.1 represents your computer's next task: producing employee paychecks. Three programs must be executed to produce the paychecks. The first program sorts and edits the input pay records, rejecting those containing invalid data and passing the good ones to the next program. The second calculates the new payroll, issues a management report, and updates the payroll master file, which is passed to the next program. The third and final program prints the paychecks. Each of the three programs is executed separately as a *job step*. Taken together, they are known as one *job*.

Figure 2.1 Job Steps to Produce Paychecks

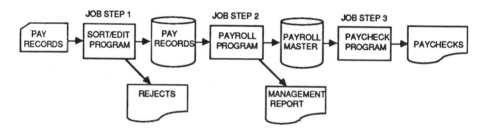

The job is DOS/VSE's basic unit of work. Whenever you want to run a program or a group of related programs such as our payroll example, you submit a job to the JCP.

Every job must have at least one job step; that is, at least one program must be executed. There is no upper limit to the number of programs (job steps) you may execute per job.

Job steps are usually related to each other by the data they process. Frequently, the output of one program is the input to the next, as in our payroll example. Unrelated programs should be run in separate jobs because if a program abends, the remainder of the job is canceled.

The collection of all jobs waiting to be processed is known as the *job stream* (see Figure 2.2). Every job you submit has a position somewhere in the job stream.

Figure 2.2 The Job Stream

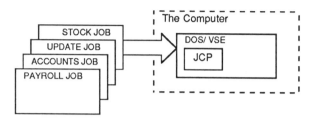

Job Syntax

Now let's turn our attention to the JCL statements that make up the job stream. As with statements in any computer language, JCL statements conform to certain syntax rules. The general format of JCL statements is:

```
//    operation        operands        comments    .
          code
```

Columns 1 and 2 contain *slashes* (//) that identify the statement as a control statement. Be sure to use forward slashes and not the backslash [\] found on some keyboards. The slashes *must* be in columns 1 and 2 and are followed by a space in column 3. You may follow the required space by more spaces if you wish.

The *operation code*, often called the *op code*, follows the space(s). It describes the type of JCL statement and the operations to be performed. The operation code may be up to seven characters in length. One or more spaces follow its last character. Some examples of operation codes are:

```
JOB

EXEC

DLBL
```

Depending on what you want to accomplish in the statement, the *operands* may be blank or may contain one or more entries separated by commas. Don't put any spaces within the operands. A space marks the end of field; everything after a space is considered a comment. The last operand of a statement must be followed by a space.

The remaining columns may be used for *comments*. The entire JCL statement must be contained between columns 1 and 71.

Here are some examples of JCL statements that follow the general format:

```
// EXEC LISTER,SIZE=80K   LISTS THE FILE
```
op   operands   comments
code

```
// EXEC PAYROLL,SIZE=AUTO
```
op   operands
code

```
// EXEC
```
op
code

Delimiter Statements

A *delimiter* prescribes the limits, or bounds, of something. JCL has three delimiter statements, which do not conform to the general format of other JCL statements. The delimiter statements are:

1. End-of-job delimiter (/&). This statement contains a slash in column 1, an ampersand in column 2, a blank in column 3, and comments (if desired) in the remaining columns. It marks the end of a job in the job stream.

2. End-of-data delimiter (/*). This statement contains a slash in column 1, an asterisk in column 2, a blank in column 3, and comments (if desired) in the remaining columns. It marks the end of a unit record file in the job stream. (Some programmers

argue that /* is not a JCL statement since it's processed by the application program, not the JCP. However, IBM includes it in the JCL reference manual, so we'll count it as a JCL statement here.)

3. End-of-procedure delimiter (/+). This statement contains a slash in column 1, a plus sign in column 2, a blank in column 3, and comments (if desired) in the remaining columns. It marks the end of a procedure in the Procedure Library.

JCL Comments

A JCL comment statement contains an asterisk (*) in column 1 (no slashes in this statement), a blank in column 2, and the text of your choice in the remaining columns. Comment statements may be placed anywhere in the job and are used for documentation. The comment appears on the operator's console while your job is executing, but the job won't stop for a response from the operator. It's unlikely the operator will read, or even notice, your comments. Use comments to document printouts of your JCL.

✓ Check Your Understanding

1. What is the minimum number of job steps you must have in a job?

2. What is the maximum number of job steps you may have in a job?

3. The queue of JCL statements waiting to be processed by the JCP is called the _____.

4. Label the four parts of the JCL statement:

[ ] [   ] [   ] [   ]

5. According to JCL syntax rules, which of the following statements are correct?

    a. `//JOB   EDITNEW    PREPARE NEW ACCOUNT RECORDS`

    b. `// EXEC   SORTEDIT,SIZE=AUTO    SORT AND EDIT RECORDS`

    c. `// EXEC,MOVEOUT`

    d. `JOB  LISTCHKS    LIST THIS MONTH'S CHECKS ISSUED`

6. Match the symbols to their descriptions.

    _____ a. /   A. End-of-procedure
    _____ b. /*   B. End-of-job
    _____ c. *   C. Comment
    _____ d. /+   D. End-of-data
                       E. End-of-job-step

✔ Answers

1. One

2. Unlimited

3. Job stream

4. //, operation code, operands, comments

5. b (*a* needs a space in column 3; *c* needs a space, not a comma, after the operation code; *d* needs slashes and a space in columns 1–3)

6. a - B; b - D; c - C; d - A

The Three Basic Statements

In this section, you'll learn how to write the three JCL statements that appear in every job: JOB, EXEC, and /&.

Let's make up a simple job to execute a program called PAYROLL that has been compiled, link edited, and cataloged to the Core Image Library as a production program:

```
// JOB PAYJOB 9999        RUN MONTHLY PAYROLL

// EXEC PAYROLL

/&
```

The first statement, the JOB statement, identifies the beginning of the job in the job stream and assigns it the name PAYJOB. The rest of the statement contains comments. The second statement, the EXEC statement, requests execution of the program named PAYROLL. The final statement, the /& delimiter, marks the end of the job.

Let's look at each of these statements in detail.

The JOB Statement

The JOB statement specifies the beginning of a job and assigns a name to it. Its format is:

```
// JOB jobname [job accounting information] [comments]
```

The operation code of the statement is JOB. Don't forget that one or more blanks must follow the word JOB.

The operand of this statement is the job's name. In our example, the operand is PAYJOB. The job name is provided by the programmer, subject to any rules or conventions of the installation.

Job names must be eight characters or fewer in length, with no spaces. These characters may be used:

Letters A through Z
Numbers 0 through 9
Special characters # $ @ / . −

Here are some valid job names:

```
/                BOBS-JOB           ACT/PAY

JOB99            MAST.UPD           SMITH
```

These job names are not valid:

BOB'SJOB   (apostrophes are not allowed)

MASTERFILEUPDATE   (must be eight or fewer characters)

LOG JOB (spaces are not allowed)

Consider the function of the job name when creating one for your job. If you and the computer operators need to discuss a job being executed, you use the job name. When printouts arrive on your desk, the printed job names help to identify them and distinguish them from other printouts. You use the job name under ICCF to view the job's status and output at your terminal. For these reasons, make your job names meaningful, unique, and as pronounceable as possible. LOCKUP is better than CLNFILES, which in turn is better than AB2CLFLS.

Many installations have additional requirements for job names, so find out what rules you must follow when you create job names.

Notice, in the format, the job accounting information in brackets and the corresponding "9999" in our sample JOB statement. This job accounting information is separated from the job name by a space because it's a comment, not an operand. The JCP doesn't process the job accounting information, but a separate program might. If your installation uses a job accounting system, the job accounting information is used to charge computer time to users. You should find out what accounting information to include in your JOB statements, if any.

Here are some valid JOB statements:

```
// JOB UPDATINV  UPDATE INVOICES
```
    job name   comments


```
// JOB INVUPDAT  D999-4C,SLB  UPDATE INVOICES
```
    job name   accounting   comments
                information


```
// JOB SORTFILE
```
    job name

Check Your Understanding

1. Write a JOB statement to identify a job as UPDATMST. Your job accounting number is X999.

2. Write a JOB statement to identify a job with your last name, no job accounting information, and a comment to the effect that this is a test run.

3. Which characters are valid in a job name?
   A - Z   ¢ $.   —   @   :   =   \   0 - 9
   #   /

✔ Answers

1. `// JOB UPDATMST X999`

2. `// JOB TEST RUN`

3. A-Z $.   —   @   0-9   #   /

The EXEC Statement

The EXECute statement (abbreviated to EXEC) requests the execution of a program or a cataloged procedure.
The formats of the EXEC statement are:

To execute a program

```
// EXEC [[PGM=]program-name]
```

To execute a cataloged procedure

```
// EXEC PROC=procname
```

Let's look first at the format to execute a *program*. When the Job Control Program encounters this statement, it passes control to the Supervisor so that the program named in the EXEC statement may be brought into a partition for execution.

The operand is PGM = program-name. "PGM = " is optional and serves only as documentation. You may omit it with no harm done. "Program-name" is the name of the program you want to execute as it is known in the Core Image Library.

Here are some sample EXEC statements:

```
// EXEC    PGM=DITTO
```

This statement calls for the program named DITTO (an IBM utility) to be executed.

```
// EXEC    PGM=LISTER
```

This statement calls for the program named LISTER to be executed.

```
// EXEC    CSORT
```

This statement calls for the program named CSORT to be executed. Notice that we omitted "PGM = ".

Why is the program name optional? When you're doing a compile-link-go job, the second step (Linkage Editor) stores the new phase temporarily in the Core Image Library under the special name ***. To execute that phase in the third step, you omit the program-name operand from the EXEC statement, as in:

```
// EXEC
```

When VSE encounters a statement like this, it looks for *** in the Core Image Library. You can do this only in a step following a link edit step in the same job, when a temporary phase named *** has been produced. Otherwise you must include an operand on the EXEC statement.

Now let's examine the format for executing a *cataloged procedure*. Remember that cataloged procedures reside in the Procedure Library. That means it's important to specify the PROC = procname operand; otherwise, the system assumes that you want to execute a program, and it searches the Core Image Library (probably in vain). For example:

```
// EXEC PROC=TESTIT    executes a procedure named
                       TESTIT from the Procedure Library
```

but

> `// EXEC TESTIT` executes a program named
> TESTIT from the Core Image Library

Figure 2.3 illustrates the difference between the two EXEC operands.

Figure 2.3 EXEC PROC= and EXEC PGM=

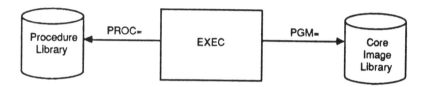

☑ **Check Your Understanding**

1. Write the statement to execute a program called UTOPIA.

2. Write the statement to execute a procedure called BRINGUP.

3. Where will the system find BRINGUP?
   Where will the system find UTOPIA?

✔ **Answers**

1. `// EXEC UTOPIA (or PGM=UTOPIA)`

2. `// EXEC PROC=BRINGUP`

3. Procedure Library; Core Image Library

The End-of-Job Statement

The End-of-Job statement marks the end of the job. The format of this statement is:

```
/&   [comments]
```

You'll recall that this is one of the three delimiter statements discussed earlier in this chapter.

When the JCP reads the /& statement, it knows the job being processed is now finished. (See Figure 2.4.)

Figure 2.4 Job and /& Separate Jobs in the Job Stream

The End-of-Job statement must contain a slash in column 1 and an ampersand in column 2. Column 3 is blank, and columns 4–71 may be used for your comments or left blank.

After reaching the /& statement and performing its end-of-job duties, the JCP attempts to read the next statement in the job stream. If the next statement is a Job Control statement, a new job begins. Jobs may follow one another continuously, which is just what happens in large production job streams. If there is not another statement following the /&, the JCP issues a message to the operator that it is ready to process a new job.

☑ Check Your Understanding

1. Code a complete job to execute a program named MAYANTE. Your accounting number is C3P0.

2. Code a complete job to execute the procedure named LIFTER. Continue using C3P0 as your accounting number.

✔ **Answers**

1. `// JOB     YOURNAME   C3P0`
    `// EXEC    MAYANTE`   or `PGM=MAYANTE`
    `/&`

2. `// JOB     YOURNAME  C3P0`
    `// EXEC    PROC=LIFTER`   `PROC=` required here
    `/&`

Instream Data

So far we've explained a simple job, to execute a program named PAYROLL. Apparently, PAYROLL requires no input data, as there is none specified for it in the job. But let's assume a more normal situation, that PAYROLL requires an input file of employee time data. Let's further assume that the program expects time cards; that is, an input unit record file in card image format, usually stored on a disk device that takes the place of a card reader. Well, that means the file must be included right in the job stream, because the job stream usually occupies the only input "card" device in a DOS/VSE installation.

Here is our sample job stream, expanded to include an instream file of data records:

```
// JOB PAYJOB 9999

// EXEC PAYROLL

433399BROWNBILL27ADEPT5404000

200185SMITHSARA77BDEPT3204012

861001JONESTOM 78CDEPT1553600

/*

/&
```

The three lines between the EXEC statement and the /* delimiter are the input file. When the EXEC statement is processed, control is given to the executing program, PAY-ROLL. The next record in the job stream (a data record) is read by the PAYROLL program, not by the JCP, when that program executes a READ instruction for the unit record file. When the program is ready to read and process the next unit record, the second data record in the stream above is read into the partition, and so on.

It's very important to include the /* statement that marks the end of the instream data. This delimiter causes the application program to execute its end-of-file routine. If you omit the /*, the program keeps on reading statements from the job stream as though they were data records, until /& is encountered. This could result in an abend or, worse, in invalid data being stored in your application files.

Figure 2.5 illustrates which program processes each statement in PAYJOB.

Figure 2.5 Processing of Statements in a Job

Statement	Processed by
// JOB PAYJOB 999	JCP
// EXEC PAYROLL	JCP
433399	PAYROLL
200185	PAYROLL
861001	PAYROLL
/*	PAYROLL
/&	JCP

If your installation has ICCF, there is an easier way to incorporate instream data into your jobs. You can bring in files that you've prepared under ICCF by using the /INCLUDE statement, which acts much like the COPY statement in a compiled language. If your installation has ICCF, you can check your ICCF manual or ask a friendly colleague for more details.

✓ Check Your Understanding

1. /& indicates that this is the end of a:
   a. Job
   b. Job step
   c. Program
   d. Procedure

2. To include instream data, you would put the input data records immediately after which of the following statements?
   a. JOB
   b. EXEC
   c. /*
   d. /&

3. Look at this job:

   ```
   // JOB    TEXTJOB
   // EXEC   PROVIT
      instream data records
   /*
   /&
   ```

   What program reads the instream data records?

4. Code a complete job to execute the program named SELECTOR, which requires an instream data file.

✔ Answers

1. a

2. b

3. PROVIT

4
   ```
   // JOB   YOURNAME
   // EXEC SELECTOR
      instream data records
   /*
   /&
   ```

Jobs with Multiple Steps

Let's look now at a multistep job that doesn't need any in-stream data:

```
// JOB ANNREPT    ANNUAL REPORT INFORMATION

// EXEC QTRINFO   PRINTS QUARTERLY REPORT

// EXEC ANNINFO   PRINTS ANNUAL REPORT

// EXEC FINSTMTS  PRINTS FINANCIAL STATEMENTS

/&
```

This job just executes programs one immediately after the other. The /& statement terminates the job.

Most jobs don't look like this because the programs need input data. Here is a multistep job that needs some information instream:

```
// JOB ANNREPT

// EXEC QTRINFO

    instream data as input to QTRINFO

/*
// EXEC ANNINFO

    instream data as input to ANNINFO

/*
// EXEC FINSTMTS
/&
```

This job places the instream data immediately after the appropriate EXEC statement. Remember that the program being executed reads the instream data until it comes to a /*, which indicates the end of the data records for that program. Figure 2.6 illustrates how this job is processed.

Figure 2.6 Processing Statements in a Multistep Job

Statement	Processed by
`// JOB ANNREPT`	JCP
`// EXEC QTRINFO`	JCP
`    instream data as input to QTRINFO`	QTRINFO
`/*`	QTRINFO
`// EXEC ANNINFO`	JCP
`    instream data as input to ANNINFO`	ANNINFO
`/*`	ANNINFO
`// EXEC FINSTMTS`	JCP
`/&`	JCP

✓ Check Your Understanding

1. How many steps are there in this job?

```
// JOB  BUYJOB
// EXEC BUYIT
123456
999XYZ
AB4932
/*
// EXEC LISTIT
* WEEKLY
* MONTHLY
* QUARTERLY
/*
// EXEC REPORT
/&
```

2. Code a job that executes first SORTER and then SELECTOR. SORTER requires instream data but SELECTOR does not.

✔ **Answers**

1. Three

2.
```
// JOB   YOURJOB
// EXEC SORTER
instream data for SORTER
/*
// EXEC SELECTOR
/&
```

What You Should Know about Your Installation

It's a good idea to ask about the information your installation requires in JOB statements. You may be assigned a job accounting number or some other identification that must always appear in your JOB statements.

You should also ask about naming conventions. Some installations have established rules about forming job names, and you should be aware of your company's requirements.

You'll also have to find out how to submit your jobs. You may be asked to use a certain queue that is run at a particular time of day or is printed on a special kind of paper.

Chapter Summary

In this chapter you've learned that each program executed within a job constitutes one job step. All the jobs waiting to be executed make up the job stream.

JCL statements conform to certain syntax rules. The general format is:

```
//  operation      operands     comments
       code
```

Four JCL statements do not follow the general format:

/&   End-of-job

/*   End-of-data

/+   End-of-procedure

*   Comments

Figure 2.7 summarizes the four statements you learned to use in this chapter.

Figure 2.7 The Basic JCL Statements

Statement	Format/Function
JOB	`// JOB jobname [accounting info] [comments]`
	Identifies and names a job and optionally provides user accounting information.
EXEC	`// EXEC [ [PGM=]programname / PROC=procname ] [comments]`
	Names a program or procedure to be executed.
End-of-data delimiter	`/* [comments]`
	Marks the end of an instream unit record file.
End-of-job delimiter	`/& [comments]`
	Marks the end of a job in the job stream.

The JOB statement specifies the beginning of a job and gives a name to the job. It may also contain job accounting information and/or comments.

The EXEC statement requests the execution of a program (EXEC) or a cataloged procedure (EXEC PROC=).

Instream data may be coded after EXEC statements; it must be followed by /*.

Multistep jobs execute one program after another. If instream data is used, you must be sure to code /* to indicate the end of the instream data for each program.

The End-of-Job statement (/&) marks the end of the job.

✓ Chapter Exercise

1. Match these terms with their descriptions.

    _____ a. Job   A. A series of jobs

    _____ b. Job step   B. The unit record data for a program

    _____ c. Job stream   C. The execution of one or more programs that accomplish a function

     D. The execution of one program or procedure

2. Identify which statements below contain format errors. Recode them to correct the errors.

    a. `//JOB PAYROLL     RUNS MONTHLY PAYCHECKS`

    b. `// JOB TSTDATA?    89411`

    c. `EXEC LISTER`

    d. `// EXEC LNKEDT`

    e. `/ / EXEC MYPROG99`

    f. `// EXEC PROC = SYSGEN`

    g. `// JOB MYPROG,9543SLB`

3. Code these statements:
   a. End-of-job
   b. End-of-instream data
   c. End-of-cataloged-procedure
   d. Beginning of comment line

4. Identify invalid job names below. Describe the error and recode the job name correctly.
   a. INVREPORT1984
   b. 76TRMENS
   c. SHARI'S
   d. RUN X
   e. TESTDATA

5. Write a complete job to execute a program called LISTIT. Make up a valid job name and use your job accounting number: C3P0. This is the second test version of the program. Indicate where any instream data records would be placed in the job stream. Include at least one comment as a separate statement in your job.

6. You have devised a job to print a report that is run every day. You've called it PRINTREP, and you've cataloged it to the Procedure Library. Code the JCL to execute this procedure.

7. Which JCL statement marks the beginning of a job?

8. Code a job to execute first LISTER, then ARRANGER, then MOVER. Each program requires an instream data set.

✔ Answers to Chapter Exercise

1. a - C; b - D; c - A

2. a. Needs a space in column 3:

   ```
   // JOB PAYROLL    RUNS MONTHLY PAYCHECKS
   ```

   b. Illegal character in job name:

   ```
   // JOB TESTDATA 89411
   ```

   c. Needs slashes and a space in columns 1–3:

   ```
   // EXEC LISTER
   ```

   d. Valid
   e. Should not have a space in column 2:

   ```
   // EXEC MYPROG99
   ```

   f. No spaces in operand:

   ```
   // EXEC PROC=SYSGEN
   ```

   g. Needs space, not comma, after job name:

   ```
   // JOB MYPROG 9543SLB
   ```

3. a. /&

   b. /*

   c. /+

   d. *

4. a. Too long; INV1984

   b. Valid

   c. No apostrophe; SHARIS

   d. No spaces; RUNX

   e. Valid

5. ```
// JOB YOURNAME C3P0
*   SECOND TEST VERSION
// EXEC LISTIT
instream data records
/*
/&
```

6. ```
// JOB   YOURNAME
// EXEC PROC=PRINTREP
/&
```

7. ```
JOB
```

8. ```
// JOB   YOURNAME
// EXEC LISTER
instream data for LISTER
/*
// EXEC ARRANGER
instream data for ARRANGER
/*
// EXEC MOVER
instream data for MOVER
/*
/&
```

chapter three

Tape Files

The jobs you created in Chapter 2 used unit-record I/O. When you use other types of I/O, you must code additional statements to tell VSE what hardware and what volumes are required. This chapter looks at the statements necessary for tape files under VSE: ASSGN (assign) and TLBL (tape label).

When you have completed this chapter, you'll be able to:

✔ Code ASSGN statements for input tape volumes

✔ Code ASSGN statements for output tape volumes

✔ Code TLBL statements for input tape files

✔ Code TLBL statements for output tape files

✔ Code complete jobs involving any combination of tape and unit-record files

✔ Indicate what happens if VSE can't find the file you've specified

Overview

Let's look at a typical job that uses card image input and tape output. Figure 3.1 diagrams this job.

Figure 3.1 Diagram of Sample Job

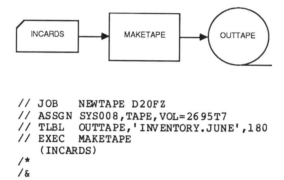

```
// JOB    NEWTAPE D20FZ
// ASSGN SYS008,TAPE,VOL=2695T7
// TLBL   OUTTAPE,'INVENTORY.JUNE',180
// EXEC   MAKETAPE
   (INCARDS)
/*
/&
```

You see some familiar statements and two new ones: ASSGN and TLBL. The ASSGN (assign) statement tells the computer what hardware device and volume are needed. In this case, we have requested tape reel 2695T7 mounted on any available tape drive. The TLBL (tape label) statement requests standard labels on the file and specifies two details for the label: the file's ID should be INVENTORY.JUNE, and it should not be erased for 180 days.

The system we're describing here is plain VSE. Many installations have added a tape handling system that makes it easier for you to create and use tape files. Find out if your installation has such a system. If so, you'll need to find out how to use it. You may need to write different statements than the ones shown here.

The ASSGN Statement

The ASSGN statement tells VSE where to find an input file or where to place an output file. It identifies the hardware unit and perhaps the tape volume. If a requested volume isn't already present, VSE asks the operator to mount it on the specified tape drive.

ASSGN identifies the tape drive by relating the file's *logical unit*, as specified in the program, to a *physical unit*. In our example, the logical unit is SYS008 and the physical unit is TAPE.

Logical Units

If you've been writing programs for your VSE system, you've already been using logical units. However, let's review them briefly.

In the following two examples, OUTTAPE is the program's name for the file, which is assigned to logical unit SYS008.

COBOL:

```
SELECT OUTTAPE
    ASSIGN TO SYS008-UT-2400-S
```

Assembler Language:

```
OUTTAPE   DTFMT     DEVADDR=SYS012,...
```

VSE has several *system logical units* with permanent assignments to physical units:

SYSRDR   The unit where the job stream resides; the JCP reads from SYSRDR

SYSIPT   The standard "card" input device; almost always assigned to the same physical unit as SYSRDR, which is why you must put "card" files in the job stream

SYSIN   A group name for SYSRDR and SYSIPT

SYSLST   The standard print device

SYSPCH   The standard "card punch" device

SYSLOG   The operator's terminal

SYSCLB   The Core Image Library

SYSSLB   The Source Statement Library

SYSRLB   The Relocatable Library

SYSLNK   Where compilers and the assembler store object modules; the Linkage Editor reads from SYSLNK

Since these logical units have standing assignments to physical units, you can use them in your programs without ASSGN statements. That's why you don't need ASSGN statements for unit record files as long as your programs assign "card" files to SYSIPT or SYSIN and print files to SYSLST. In Chapter 2, we assumed that all input "card" files were assigned to SYSIPT and all output print files were assigned to SYSLST.

Your tape and disk files are typically assigned to *programmer logical units* named SYS*nnn*. Many installations have made some permanent assignments for programmer logical units as well. For example, SYS007 may be permanently assigned to a particular tape unit, SYS008 to another tape unit, SYS009 to a particular disk volume, and SYS010 to another disk volume. If you want to use those permanent assignments, use the appropriate logical units in your program and you don't need ASSGN statements. But you'll need to use nonstandard assignments some of the time.

Physical Units

If your installation has only one type of tape unit, or if you don't care which type of unit is assigned to your file, you can use a generalized assignment like this:

```
ASSGN SYS008,TAPE
```

VSE will assign the first available tape unit to your file. This is the most general and flexible hardware assignment. It's the best one to use as long as any tape unit in the installation will do.

If your installation has more than one type of tape unit and you want to select a particular type, you can do it with a statement like this:

```
ASSGN SYS008,2400
```

where 2400 is one type of tape unit. VSE will assign the first available 2400 tape unit to the file associated with SYS008. This is the best style of hardware assignment when you do care which type of drive is used.

Let's look briefly at some other ways to specify the physical device.

ASSGN SYS008,181

Every device attached to the CPU has a three-digit address. Here we've used an address for a particular tape drive. This causes the job to be delayed until the drive at address 181 is available, unless the operator assigns it to another unit.

ASSGN SYS008,(181, 182, 183)

This lets VSE choose from a list of device addresses. It's a little more flexible than specifying just one address.

ASSGN SYS008,SYSLST

This tells VSE to use the same device that's assigned to another logical unit, in this case SYSLST.

Most of the time, you'll specify either TAPE if your system has only one type of drive or the drive type if it has multiple types. Limiting your job by specifying address(es) or another logical unit should be done only if an unusual case requires it.

The VOL Parameter

Most tape volumes have an internal label called VOL1 that identifies and describes the volume to the system. VOL1 includes a volume serial number. For VSE to find your input tape file (if you don't have a tape handling system), you must tell it what volume to use by specifying VOL = volume-serial-number on the ASSGN statement. For example:

```
// ASSGN SYS008,TAPE,VOL=546829
```

This requests that volume 546829 be mounted on any available tape drive and assigned to logical unit SYS008.

Obviously, you must specify VOL for input files. Do you need it for output files? Ordinarily, no; let the operator select a new or scratch volume for you. However, if you must use an application's private volume, then you specify VOL for the output file.

Summary of the ASSGN Statement

Figure 3.2 shows the basic format of the ASSGN statement. The logical unit comes from the program and begins with SYS. The physical unit indicates the type of hardware to be used. VOL indicates the serial number of the desired tape volume. Other parameters are available, but these are the most common ones.

Figure 3.2 Format of ASSGN

```
// ASSGN logical-unit,physical-unit[,VOL=volume-serial-number]
```

This statement involves two types of parameters: positional and keyword. The system recognizes positional parameters by their physical location in the statement. Thus, the first value (all characters preceding the first comma) is always interpreted as the logical unit, while the second value is always interpreted as the physical unit. If you coded:

```
// ASSGN   TAPE,SYS007
```

a human reader would recognize that the values are reversed since TAPE is a physical unit and SYS007 is a logical unit, but the JCP can't make that kind of assumption. The JCP would reject the statement because there is no logical unit named TAPE; it would never examine the second parameter.

A keyword parameter differs from a positional parameter because it has a key word followed by an equal sign. In Figure 3.2, VOL= is a keyword parameter. The JCP identifies these parameters by their key words, not their positions. As a result, keyword parameters may appear in any order. However, they must never take up a positional parameter's location. Thus, keyword parameters follow positional parameters.

ASSGN for Input Tape Files

An input file should be assigned to a device capable of reading it and should be identified by volume serial number. Here are some examples:

```
// ASSGN SYS007,2400,VOL=160027
// ASSGN SYS007,TAPE,VOL=165027
```

The first example specifies the type of tape drive, while the second example doesn't. The second example should be used only in shops with just one type of tape drive.

ASSGN for Output Tape Files

An output file should be assigned to whatever type of device is most appropriate to the application, with the analyst or designer usually making this decision. Don't specify VOL unless a private volume is called for. Here are some examples:

```
// ASSGN SYS008,TAPE
// ASSGN SYS008,2400
```

Your unit record files also need ASSGN statements if your program does not assign them to the system logical units SYSIPT, SYSLST, SYSPCH, etc.

Whatever assignment you make lasts until the job terminates or you enter another ASSGN statement for the same logical unit.

When and Where to Use ASSGN

Every file must have an ASSGN statement unless your program assigns it to a logical unit with a permanent assignment at your installation. By the time the JCP encounters the EXEC statement, it must know where all the files are. So put all your ASSGN statements before the EXEC statement they pertain to.

Resetting Assignments: The RESET Statement

The assignments you make with the ASSGN statement are temporary. They are cleared (reset to the standard assignment) by the /& statement at the end of the job. You can make a permanent assignment, often called a *hard assignment,* with the ASSGN statement; but since you shouldn't do that without coordinating with the operator and management, we're not even going to show you how.

You don't have to wait until the job ends to reset assignments. You can reset all units to their standard assignments with this statement:

```
// RESET ALL
```

This clears all preceding ASSGN statements in the job.

In the best of all possible worlds, where you never make any mistakes, you would never need the RESET statement. But some programmers make a few mistakes, so let's look at what can happen without resetting assignments. Here's a fairly simple job:

```
// JOB MAKELIST R2D2
// TLBL INFILE,'MARKET.DATA.CHI'
// EXEC TPRINT
/&
```

The program named TPRINT uses an input tape file (INFILE) on SYS007. At our installation, SYS007 has a permanent assignment, so we don't need an ASSGN statement for it. So far, so good.

Now let's do something that programmers do all the time: let's modify the job to meet a new situation. We'll add a step:

```
// JOB MAKELIST R2D2
// ASSGN SYS006,TAPE,VOL=145007
// ASSGN SYS007,SYSLST
// TLBL INTAPE,'CAMPAIGN.DATA.CHI'
// EXEC SELECT
*  END OF FIRST STEP
// TLBL INFILE,'MARKET.DATA.CHI'
// EXEC TPRINT
/&
```

The first step uses an input file on SYS006 and an output print file on SYS007. Notice the statement that assigns SYS007 to SYSLST.

Now we get to the second step. It's still expecting SYS007 to have its standard tape unit assignment. (We forgot that, since the JCL doesn't mention SYS007.) We neglected to add an ASSGN or RESET statement for it, so it's still assigned to SYSLST. The result: an error message requiring operator intervention.

The easiest solution is to add a RESET statement after the first EXEC statement. In fact, some programmers routinely include a RESET statement at the end of every step, even the last step, to prevent future problems if a step is added.

✓ Check Your Understanding

You will use this job:

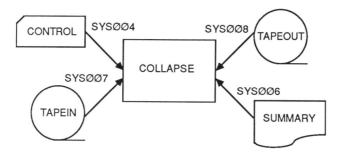

1. Notice that the file named CONTROL is assigned to SYS004. Code a statement to assign it to the same physical unit as SYSIPT.

2. Code a statement to assign TAPEIN to any available 2400 tape drive. TAPEIN is on volume 843019.

3. Code a statement to assign TAPEOUT to any available tape reel on any available tape drive.

4. Code a statement to assign SUMMARY to the same physical unit as SYSLST.

5. How long will these assignments last?
   a. Until another ASSGN statement or RESET statement changes them or the end of the job
   b. Until the end of the day
   c. Until another job changes them

6. Code a statement to reset all previous ASSGN statements in the job.

✔ Answers

1. `// ASSGN SYS004,SYSIPT`

2. `// ASSGN SYS007,2400,VOL=843019`

3. `// ASSGN SYS008,TAPE`

4. `// ASSGN SYS006,SYSLST`

5. a

6. `// RESET ALL`

The TLBL Statement

You've already seen how the tape reel is identified by the volume label (VOL1) that you reference in the ASSGN VOL= parameter. Each file on a standard reel also has its own label (HDR1) containing pertinent information about the file. The TLBL (Tape LaBeL) statement refers to the HDR1 label. If the file has standard file labels, you must code a TLBL statement in addition to the ASSGN statement.

TLBL for Input Files

For input files, TLBL needs just a couple of parameters. The label already exists, and you want VSE to check it.

The first parameter gives the *program's* name for the file to tell VSE which file you're talking about. In these examples, the program's filename is OLDFILE.

COBOL:

```
SELECT INPUT-TAPE-FILE
    ASSIGN TO SYS007-UT-2400-S-OLDFILE.
```

Assembler:

```
OLDFILE    DTFMT DEVADDR=SYS007,...
```

The TLBL statement for this file begins like this:

```
// TLBL OLDFILE,...
```

The second parameter gives the file's ID, up to 17 characters, as it appears in the tape label. You might think of this as the file's *real* name. Enclose it in single quotes in the TLBL statement, like this:

```
// TLBL OLDFILE,'INVENTORY.JUNE.86'
```

If you omit the file ID, VSE doesn't check it on the label; this could be dangerous, so always include the ID for labeled input files.

The filename and file ID are all you need for most input tape files, but other parameters can be specified if you want VSE to check them in HDR1. Figure 3.3 shows the full format of the TLBL statement. Let's look at how the remaining parameters are used for an input file.

Figure 3.3 TLBL Format

```
// TLBL file-name,[file-ID],[date],[file-serial-number],
       [volume-sequence-number],[file-sequence-number],
       [generation-number],[version-number]
```

The date causes VSE to check the creation date in the header label. This helps to select a particular version of a file when several exist. Use Julian format: yy/ddd.

The file serial number should be the same as the volume serial number on the ASSGN statement. If you code it here, VSE checks it in the file's header label. Since that matches the serial number on the volume's header label, one check should suffice.

A large data file may occupy several reels of tape. All the volumes making up one file are sequentially numbered in the file header label. Your VOL parameter specifies which volume to start with, but you can ask VSE to confirm the sequence number by coding the volume sequence number in the TLBL statement. VSE checks the sequence number in the file header label and, if it doesn't match the TLBL statement, VSE asks the operator what to do.

A tape volume may contain several files. The file sequence number indicates a file's position on a multifile reel. The default is 1. This book deals only with single-file reels, so we won't use this parameter.

When you make a major revision to a master file, keeping the same file ID, a new *generation* is created. A minor revision creates a new *version*. The header label includes generation and version numbers so you can make sure you're working with the most recent version of the data. To do so, specify the generation number and the version number on the TLBL statement. If you don't, the generation and version of the current file are assumed to be correct.

Coding Positional Parameters

All the parameters shown in Figure 3.3 are positional. The ones in brackets are optional. If you want to omit an optional parameter, you must code its comma to mark its position. Otherwise, the JCP misinterprets the parameters that follow it. You don't need to code commas after the last parameter you're including.

Suppose you want to code all parameters but the file serial number and the file sequence number. Your statement would look like this:

```
// TLBL TAPETRAN,'TRANSACTS.90216',87/132,,1,,3,4
```

The extra commas are critical as they tell the JCP that two parameters are omitted.

Suppose you want to omit the date and the volume sequence number, as well. Your statement would look like this:

```
// TLBL TAPETRAN,'TRANSACTS.90216',,,,,3,4
```

Those five commas in a row may look funny to you now, but you'll get used to them.

If you also want to omit the generation and version numbers, life is easier:

```
// TLBL TAPETRAN,'TRANSACTS.90216'
```

You don't need any commas after the last parameter you use.

Summary of TLBL for Input

By way of summary, let's look at some sample TLBL statements for input files.

```
// TLBL LOCKIN,'ACCTS.RECV.MAY'
```

This is usually enough to identify the file you want to use. The program calls the file LOCKIN; the name in the file's label is ACCTS.RECV.MAY.

```
// ASSGN SYS007,2400,VOL=6349T1
// TLBL PARTSINV,'PARTS.PLANT5',,,3
```

This asks VSE to confirm that volume 6349T1 is the third volume in the PARTS.PLANT5 file before opening it for processing. The first two volumes are being skipped for some reason. The volume serial number is sufficient to locate the file, but using the volume sequence number on TLBL acts as a double-check. Note the commas indicating missing positional parameters.

```
// ASSGN SYS007,2400,VOL=400116
// TLBL MERGE1,'FOREIGN.ACCTS',86/300,,,,7,4
```

Here we want to use the fourth version of the seventh generation of FOREIGN.ACCTS. It should be on volume 400116, but we ask VSE to confirm the creation date, generation number, and version number before opening the file.

 Check Your Understanding

Use this job in the following questions:

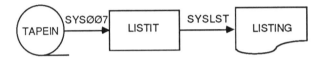

1. Suppose you want to list the file labeled FORCED.PLANTS in the header label. Code the TLBL statement.

   ```
   // ASSGN SYS007,2400,VOL=630209
   ```

2. What happens if volume 630209 contains a file named FORCED.BULBS not FORCED.PLANTS?
   a. VSE asks the operator what to do.
   b. VSE rejects the file and terminates the job.
   c. VSE issues a warning message and uses the file.

3. Revise your statement to confirm that the file was created on the 163rd day of 1985.

4. What happens if the file named FORCED.PLANTS on volume 630209 was created on the 100th day of 1985?
   a. VSE asks the operator what to do.
   b. VSE rejects the file and cancels the job.
   c. VSE ignores the creation date and uses the file; the TLBL creation date is just for documentation.

5. Revise your statement to confirm that this is the 16th version of the 32nd generation of the file.

6. What happens if FORCED.PLANTS on volume 630209 is the first version of the first generation?
   a. VSE asks the operator what to do.
   b. VSE rejects the file and cancels the job.
   c. VSE ignores the generation and version numbers and uses the file anyway.

7. Suppose instead you want to list MEMBERS.CALIF. This is a multivolume file and you want to be sure to start with the first volume. Code the TLBL statement.

8. What happens if the specified volume is the *second* volume of MEMBERS.CALIF?
   a. VSE asks the operator what to do.
   b. VSE rejects the file and terminates the job with an appropriate error message.
   c. VSE uses the file anyway; the TLBL file sequence number is just for documentation.

9. Why specify extra TLBL parameters such as creation date and version number?
   a. They help protect against the wrong files being used.
   b. They are used to update the file's header label.
   c. They don't make any difference, so you might as well use them.

✔ Answers

1. `// TLBL TAPEIN,'FORCED.PLANTS'`

2. a

3. `// TLBL TAPEIN,'FORCED.PLANTS',85/163`

4. a

5. `// TLBL TAPEIN,'FORCED.PLANTS',85/163,,,,32,16`

6. a

7. `// TLBL TAPEIN,'MEMBERS.CALIF',,,1`

8. a

9. a

TLBL for Output Files

When a tape file is being created, the TLBL parameters provide information for the label, as shown in Figure 3.4.

Figure 3.4 TLBL for Output

Parameter	Meaning
File ID	The file's internal name; up to 17 characters
Date	The expiration date if expressed as yy/ddd; number of days to retain if expressed as *nnnn;* the default is zero (no retention)
Volume serial number	Don't use this parameter; VSE will provide it for the label
Volume sequence number	This volume's position in the file; VSE provides this value automatically unless you override it for some reason
File sequence number	This file's position on the volume; the default is 1
Generation number	This generation's number; the default is blank
Version number	This version's number; the default is blank

Only the date parameter is truly different from input to output. On input it asks VSE to confirm the *creation* date. On output it gives the *expiration* date, the date after which the file may be erased. If you provide a retention period, VSE calculates the expiration date for the label.

Let's look at some sample jobs using output tapes.

```
// ASSGN SYS008,2400
// TLBL TAPEOUT,'PAYROLL.BACKUP',100
```

This tape will be created on a 2400 tape unit. The program calls it TAPEOUT, but its internal name is PAYROLL.BACKUP. It should be retained 100 days. The operator will select the volume(s) for it, and VSE will provide the file sequence number and volume sequence number as appropriate. Generation and version numbers will not be used. This is the most common style of TLBL statement when not creating a generation data set.

```
// ASSGN SYS007,2400
// TLBL TAPEIN,'PERSONNEL.VAULT',,,,,3,6
// ASSGN SYS008,2400
// TLBL TAPEOUT,'PERSONNEL.VAULT',30,,,,3,7
```

Here we're working with a generation data set called PER-SONNEL.VAULT. Both the input and the output files are shown so you can compare them. We're making a minor revision, so we're going from version 3.6 to 3.7.

✓ Check Your Understanding

You will work with this job:

1. Code the TLBL statement to call the output tape JUNEMAS-TER. Let the retention period default to zero.

```
// ASSGN SYS007,3240,VOL=134900
// TLBL TAPEIN,'MAYMASTER'
// ASSGN SYS008,3240
```

2. Revise your statement to specify a 60-day retention period.

3. Revise your statement to specify the last day of 1989 as the expiration date.

4. Add a TLBL statement to the job below so version 7.0 of PROCEDURES is created. It should be retained 6 months.

```
// ASSGN SYS007,3240,VOL=146500
// TLBL TAPEIN,'PROCEDURES',,,,,6,4
// ASSGN SYS008,3240
```

✔ Answers

1. `// TLBL TAPEOUT,'JUNEMASTER'`

2. `// TLBL TAPEOUT,'JUNEMASTER',60`

3. `// TLBL TAPEOUT,'JUNEMASTER',89/365`

4. `// TLBL TAPEOUT,'PROCEDURES',180,,,,7,0`

Chapter Summary

Figure 3.5 summarizes the ASSGN and TLBL statements for input and output files, showing when parameters are optional and when they're required. Spend a few moments examining the chart and making sure you understand how each parameter works. Don't forget you can always refer back to this chart when writing JCL for tape files.

Suppose you are listing a tape file using a program called LISTIT. Here's what the JCL might look like:

```
// JOB LISTTAPE R2D2
// ASSGN SYS007,TAPE,VOL=PRR2D2
// TLBL INFILE,'ERRORS.PAYRUN',86/160
// EXEC LISTIT
/&
```

The input file is named ERRORS.PAYRUN, was created on the 160th day of 1986, and is on volume PRR2D2. The program calls this file INFILE and assigns it to SYS007. Any tape unit in the installation will do. No special statements are needed for the listing file because the program assigns it to SYSLST.

Now suppose you're creating an output tape from an input "card" file.

```
// JOB MAKETAPE R2D2
// ASSGN SYS008,TAPE
// TLBL OUTFILE,'CUSTS.NEW.JUNE',60
// EXEC CARDTAPE
instream records go here
/*
/&
```

Here a new tape named CUSTS.NEW.JUNE is to be retained 60 days. The program (CARDTAPE) calls this file OUTFILE and assigns it to SYS008. Notice that the ASSGN and TLBL statements precede the EXEC statement but the instream unit-record file follows it.

Now let's look at a job that copies a tape.

```
// JOB JUNEBACK R2D2
// ASSGN SYS007,TAPE,VOL=534000
// ASSGN SYS008,TAPE
// TLBL TAPEIN,'CUSTS.NEW.JUNE'
// TLBL TAPEOUT,'BACKUP.JUNE',60
// EXEC COPYTAPE
/&
```

Figure 3.5 Summary of Tape I/O Statements

	Input	Output
ASSGN Statement	Required if the program relates the file to a logical unit without a permanent physical assignment.	Same as input.
logical-unit	Required; must match program.	Required; must match program.
physical-unit	Required; be as general as possible.	Required; be as general as possible.
VOL	Required unless you're positive the desired volume will be on the indicated physical unit.	Omit unless the application requires a specific volume be used.
TLBL Statement	Required if the file has standard labels; otherwise omit.	Required if you want the file to have standard labels; otherwise omit.
filename	Required; must match program.	Required; must match program.
file-ID	Recommended to force VSE to check the file-ID in the label.	Recommended; otherwise VSE puts the filename in the label.
date	Optional; include if you want VSE to check the creation date.	Recommended; otherwise the file expires immediately and VSE might erase it before it's dismounted.
file-serial-number	Omit; the same as ASSGN . . . VOL.	Omit; the same as ASSGN . . . VOL; let VSE provide this parameter.
volume-sequence-number	Optional; include if you want VSE to check this parameter in the label.	Omit; let VSE provide this parameter (unless you have a strong reason to override it).
file-sequence-number	Optional.	Optional.
generation-number	Optional; use only if you want VSE to check this parameter in the label.	Required if you want a nonblank value in the label.
version-number	Same as above.	Same as above.

First we describe the input file, CUSTS.NEW.JUNE, on volume 534000. COPYTAPE calls this file TAPEIN and assigns it to SYS007. Then we describe the output file, BACKUP.JUNE, which is to be retained for 60 days. COPYTAPE calls this file TAPEOUT and assigns it to SYS008. Notice here that all the ASSGN and TLBL statements precede the EXEC statement. We like to put the ASSGN statements first.

Our next job is considerably more complex. We're going to use transaction "cards" to update a customer master tape file, which is then used as input to a report program.

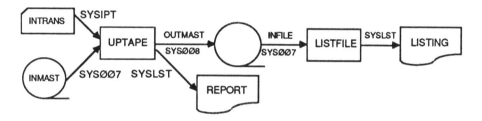

The job has two steps and the updated tape is passed from the first to the second step.

```
// JOB UPDATE R2D2
// ASSGN SYS007,TAPE,VOL=416000
// ASSGN SYS008,TAPE
// TLBL INMAST,'CUSTOMER.MAST',86/032,,,,7,0
// TLBL OUTMAST,'CUSTOMER.MAST',200,,,,8,0
// EXEC UPTAPE
(INTRANS records go here)
/*
// ASSGN SYS007,TAPE
// TLBL INFILE,'CUSTOMER.MAST',,,,,8,0
// EXEC LISTFILE
/&
```

In the first step, all the ASSGN and TLBL statements precede the EXEC statement. Notice that we're going from generation 7.0 to 8.0 of CUSTOMER.MAST. The instream data records for INTRANS follow the EXEC statement.

After the end-of-data delimiter, the second step begins with the ASSGN and TLBL statements for INFILE. We have *not* specified a volume serial number for this input file because we don't know what it is, but we do know that it's already mounted, having just been created in the preceding step. Even though we have specified neither the exact address of the tape unit nor the exact volume number, VSE will be able to find the tape. If we had not specified the generation number, however, VSE would not know which version of CUSTOMER.MAST to use.

Don't forget that your installation might have a tape-handling system and also might have some permanent tape unit assignments you can take advantage of.

✅ Chapter Exercise

For this exercise, assume your installation has several 2400 tape drives and several 3420 tape drives. Use 3420 drives unless otherwise specified. Your accounting code is C3P0.

All actual filenames and volume numbers are shown beneath the tape reels in the job diagrams.

1. Code the JCL for this job. Give NEW.ITEMS a 30-day retention period.

2. Suppose MAKESEQ assigns NEWRECS to SYS001 instead of SYSIPT. Adapt the above job to reflect this change.

3. Code the JCL for this job.

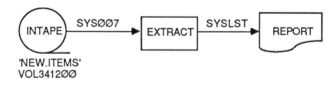

4. Adapt the above job to make sure you use the version of NEW.ITEMS created on the 200th day of 1990.

5. Suppose EXTRACT assigns REPORT to SYS002 instead of to SYSLST. Adapt your job to reflect this change.

6. Code the JCL for the job shown below, which creates a new generation of the tape file. RESTORE.COMP was created by a 2400, but the new tape should be created by a 3420. Set a 100-day retention period on the output tape.

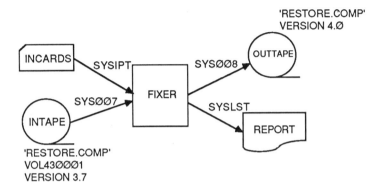

7. What happens if the file on volume 430001 is version 3.6 of RESTORE.COMP?
    a. VSE asks the operator what to do.
    b. VSE uses the file anyway.
    c. VSE rejects the file and terminates the job.
    d. VSE runs the program but creates INTAPE as end-of-file.

✔ Answers to Chapter Exercise

1.
```
// JOB MAKESEQ C3P0
// ASSGN SYS007,3420
// TLBL SEQRECS,'NEW.ITEMS',30
// EXEC MAKESEQ
(NEWRECS goes here)
/*
/&
```

2. Add a statement like this to the job:

```
// ASSGN SYS001,SYSIPT
```

3.
```
// JOB EXTAPE C3P0
// ASSGN SYS007,3420,VOL=341200
// TLBL INTAPE,'NEW.ITEMS'
// EXEC EXTRACT
/&
```

4. Change the TLBL statement to:

```
// TLBL INTAPE,'NEW.ITEMS',90200
```

5. Add a statement like this to the job:

```
// ASSGN SYS002,SYSLST
```

6.
```
// JOB FIXTAPE C3P0
// ASSGN SYS007,2400,VOL=430001
// TLBL INTAPE,'RESTORE.COMP',,,,,3,7
// ASSGN SYS008,3420
// TLBL OUTTAPE,'RESTORE.COMP',,,,,4,0
// EXEC FIXER
(INCARDS go here)
/*
/&
```

7. a

chapter four

VSAM Data Sets

The previous chapter showed you how to use tape files in your jobs. Now it's time to look at DASD (Direct Access Storage Device) files.

Today's installations generally use two DASD access methods: SAM (Sequential Access Method) and VSAM (Virtual Storage Access Method). Two earlier methods, DAM (Direct Access Method) and ISAM (Indexed Sequential Access Method), rarely appear nowadays. VSAM files are the easiest to code JCL for, so we'll cover those first. You'll learn how to use SAM files in Chapter Five.

When you have completed this chapter, you will be able to:

✔ Code a DLBL statement for an input VSAM data set in the master catalog

✔ Code a DLBL statement for an output VSAM data set in the master catalog

✔ Code a DLBL statement for an input VSAM data set in a user catalog

✔ Code a DLBL statement for an output VSAM data set in a user catalog

✔ Code a DLBL statement for a job catalog

✔ Code a complete job involving VSAM data sets

✔ Code a complete job involving a job catalog and several VSAM data sets

VSAM Background

You may already be familiar with VSAM from your programming experience, but let's go over some features that are important in JCL. Refer to the diagram in Figure 4.1.

Figure 4.1 VSAM Data Management Structure

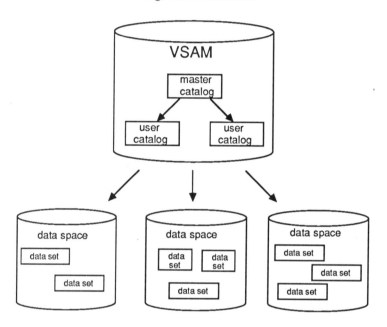

Disk storage space under the control of VSAM is called *data space*. Within this data space reside the *data sets* (files) VSAM manages. Both data sets and unused data space are recorded in VSAM's catalogs. VSAM uses the information in its catalogs to create, access, and manipulate data sets.

A VSAM catalog contains all the information the system needs in order to find a data set. Your JCL must provide the data set's name, and VSAM does the rest.

To avoid overcrowded catalogs, VSAM allows the use of multiple catalogs. This practice decentralizes control and increases the system's efficiency. VSAM requires that one catalog be designated as the Master Catalog; it points to the other catalogs, known as *user catalogs*.

New VSAM data sets must be defined through Access Methods Services (AMS) so that catalog entries exist and data space is reserved before any job can write data in them. If you don't know how to define new VSAM data sets, see your local VSAM expert. This book does not cover Access Methods Services. As far as JCL is concerned, all VSAM data sets, whether input or output, already exist.

VSE Advanced Functions 2 lets you place SAM files in VSAM data space. VSAM manages the SAM files just as if they were VSAM files. This makes it easier for you to create and access the SAM files.

Sample VSAM Job

Let's say you want to process a job using a VSAM file as input (see Figure 4.2).

Figure 4.2 VSAM Input File

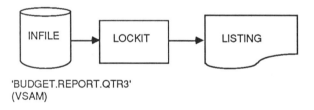

'BUDGET.REPORT.QTR3'
(VSAM)

The only output is a printed report; you'll use the standard assignment for the printer, so no JCL statements are needed for the output. You do, however, need a DLBL (Disk LaBeL) statement so the system can locate your input file on the disk device. The job would look like this:

```
// JOB SAMPLE
// DLBL INFILE,'BUDGET.REPORT.QTR3',,VSAM,CAT=ACCAT
// EXEC LOCKIT,SIZE=AUTO
/&
```

When the VSAM file BUDGET.REPORT.QTR3 was defined, all the necessary information regarding its size and location was automatically placed into VSAM's catalog. This means that no ASSGN statements are needed—the system already has that information. All you need to access a VSAM file is the DLBL statement.

Here is the format for the DLBL used for files under the control of VSAM:

```
// DLBL filename,'file-ID',[date],VSAM[,CAT=filename]
```

The first four parameters are positional and must appear in this order. If the date is omitted, you must code its comma to show that it's missing. The keyword parameter lets you specify a user catalog. We'll explain later where AMS looks for the data set if you omit this parameter. (Our format omits some keyword parameters that are rarely used.)

Now let's look at how we coded our SAMPLE job. INFILE is the *filename*. This is how the file is known to us in the ASSIGN clause (COBOL) or DCL statement (PL/I) in the source program. In Assembler, the filename is given in the Access Method Control Block (ACB) rather than in a DTF. The filename is always required.

'BUDGET.REPORT.QTR3' is the *file-ID*. File-ID is the name placed into the VSAM catalog when the file is defined. This is how the file is known to VSAM.

The pair of commas following the file-ID indicates an omitted operand, the *date*. For VSAM files, the date operand is used only for output files. In this example, because we're dealing with an input file, we omit the date operand and indicate the omission with a comma.

The next operand, VSAM, is the *code*. The code tells the system that we are using a VSAM file. There are other codes for other types of files; you'll learn about them in the next chapter.

The CAT = ACCAT operand specifies that the data set is owned by the user catalog named ACCAT.

Now let's look at the EXEC statement of our SAMPLE job.

```
// EXEC PRINTIT,SIZE=AUTO
```

For any programs using VSAM files, be sure to use the parameter SIZE = AUTO on your EXEC statements. SIZE = AUTO means that the system calculates automatically the amount of partition space your compiled program requires for execution. If you omit the SIZE parameter, the entire partition is allocated to the program, and no space is left for the system programs VSAM needs to process the application program. (Under certain circumstances, SIZE=AUTO won't yield the desired results and the job will fail. Then you'll have to figure out the correct size and code it yourself, as in SIZE=58K. If this happens to you, get help from a local expert.)

✓ Check Your Understanding

Write a job having a VSAM file as input and a printed report as output.

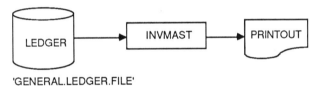

'GENERAL.LEDGER.FILE'

The file is known to VSAM as GENERAL.LEDGER.FILE and is owned by the ACCAT catalog.

✔ Answer

```
// JOB VSAMJOB
// DLBL LEDGER,'GENERAL.LEDGER.FILE',,VSAM,CAT=ACCAT
// EXEC INVMAST,SIZE=AUTO
/&
```

Output VSAM Files

Let's change our example. Instead of printing a report, we're going to write the data as output to another VSAM data set (see Figure 4.3).

Figure 4.3 VSAM Input and Output Files

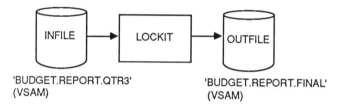

'BUDGET.REPORT.QTR3'
(VSAM)

'BUDGET.REPORT.FINAL'
(VSAM)

Now the job looks like this:

```
// JOB SAMPLE
// DLBL INFILE,'BUDGET.REPORT.QTR3',,VSAM,CAT=ACCAT
// DLBL OUTFILE,'BUDGET.REPORT.FINAL',90,VSAM,CAT=ACCAT
// EXEC LOCKIT,SIZE=AUTO
/&
```

The DLBL for the output data set is similar to the input data set's DLBL. The filename is OUTFILE to agree with the source program. The file-ID is the name entered into the VSAM catalog when the new file was defined (using Access Methods Services). Now we have "90" in the date operand so that the data set will be retained for 90 days. You may specify the date operand as a number of days (0 through 9999) or as a specific expiration date (in the format yy/ddd). If you specify a date, it overrides the expiration date given in the catalog.

The order of DLBL statements in this job is not important, so long as both precede the EXEC statement. We tend to put the input files first and the output files last.

Check Your Understanding

1. Change the last job you coded to write the output [POSTED] to a disk data set named INV.MASTER. Keep the output until the last day of 1990. Continue using the ACCAT catalog.

2. What happens to your job if you use instream data as input and keep your same VSAM file for output? Rewrite the previous exercise to accommodate instream data records instead of an input data set. Use the expiration date defined for the VSAM data set. (Don't forget that instream data *follows* the EXEC statement.)

✔ **Answers**

```
1. // JOB VSAMJOB
   // DLBL LEDGER,'GENERAL.LEDGER.FILE',,VSAM,CAT=ACCAT
   // DLBL POSTED,'INV.MASTER',90/365,VSAM,CAT=ACCAT
   // EXEC INVMAST,SIZE=AUTO
   /&
```

```
2. // JOB VSAMJOB
   // DLBL POSTED,'INV.MASTER',,VSAM,CAT=ACCAT
   // EXEC INVMAST,SIZE=AUTO
   data records
   /*
   /&
```

User Catalogs

The CAT= operand names the user catalog that controls the data set. Most installations assign all their data sets to user catalogs; the master catalog points only to user catalogs and controls no other data sets.

In the operand CAT=ACCAT, the value ACCAT refers to a DLBL statement that defines the user catalog. The DLBL statement must either be included in the job or be stored in the system's permanent label area. You can assume that all your user catalogs have been permanently defined in the system's label area, so all you have to do is get the correct value in your CAT= operand, and VSAM will find the catalog and the data set.

Job Catalogs

Suppose that you have a large job to run, and all its data sets are controlled by the same user catalog. A user catalog controlling all (or most of) the data sets for a job is known as a *job catalog*.

To establish a job catalog, code a DLBL statement for filename IJSYSUC. IJSYSUC is a system-assigned logical unit. The DLBL for a job catalog named ACCTG.JOB.CAT would look like this:

```
// DLBL IJSYSUC,'ACCTG.JOB.CAT',,VSAM
```

Put the IJSYSUC DLBL before the other DLBLs in the job.

When you use a job catalog, that catalog (instead of the master catalog) is searched for all VSAM data sets in your job that don't have a CAT= operand. Thus, you don't need the CAT= operand except for data sets not in the job catalog.

✓ Check Your Understanding

1. Change the following user catalog to a job catalog. USER3's name is PERSONL.CATALOG.

```
// JOB SAMPLE5
// DLBL TESTIN,'TEST.FILE.1',,VSAM,CAT=USER3
// DLBL TESTOUT,'TEST.FILE.2',,VSAM,CAT=USER3
// EXEC TESTPROG,SIZE=AUTO
/&
```

2. Suppose the job uses a second output data set (ERRORS) that should go in 'OPTIONAL.TEST.FILE' owned by USER2 catalog. Revise your job.

✔ Answers

1.
```
// JOB SAMPLE5
// DLBL IJSYSUC,'PERSONL.CATALOG',,VSAM
// DLBL TESTIN,'TEST.FILE.1',,VSAM
// DLBL TESTOUT,'TEST.FILE.2',,VSAM
// EXEC TESTPROG,SIZE=AUTO
/&
```

Remember that when you specify a job catalog, that catalog is searched for all data sets not having the CAT= operand. Neither file above has a CAT = operand, so VSAM will search the job catalog for both files.

2.
```
// JOB SAMPLE5
// DLBL IJSYSUC,'PERSONL.CATALOG',,VSAM
// DLBL TESTIN,'TEST.FILE.1',,VSAM
// DLBL TESTOUT,'TEST.FILE.2',,VSAM
// DLBL ERRORS,'OPTIONAL.TEST.FILE',,VSAM,CAT=USER2
// EXEC TESTPROG,SIZE=AUTO
/&
```

Since the fourth DLBL statement has a CAT= parameter, the system will search USER2, not the job catalog, for OPTIONAL.TEST.FILE.

SAM under VSAM

Much like a foster child, SAM files may take up residence in VSAM's data space. VSAM catalogs the SAM files and manages their space for you, making these files much more convenient to access than regular SAM files. Use these files just like other VSAM files.

Permanent DLBLs

Your installation may store some permanent DLBLs for its major data sets. For example, the master inventory, master customer, and master employee databases probably have permanent DLBLs. Your jobs don't need to include DLBL statements for these files as long as the programs refer to them by the right names. Take some time to find out what permanent DLBLs your installation has and what names your programs can use to refer to them.

Chapter Summary

VSAM processing is so automated that you need specify only a DLBL statement to access a VSAM data set.

```
// DLBL filename,file-ID,[date],VSAM[,CAT=filename]
```

The date pertains only to output files and overrides the expiration date defined through AMS. CAT= specifies a catalog other than the job catalog (or the master catalog when there is no job catalog).

Define a job catalog if several data sets in the job are owned by the same user catalog. This definition should precede the DLBLs that use it.

```
// DLBL IJSYSUC,file-ID,,VSAM
```

Access existing SAM-under-VSAM files just like VSAM files.

Always specify SIZE=AUTO on any EXEC statement for a program using VSAM data sets.

You don't need DLBL statements for data sets with permanent DLBL definitions.

 **Chapter Exercise**

1. Write a DLBL statement for an input file known to the program as NEWIDS. Use a VSAM file named TEMP.IDS.XMAS.ERIE in the ERIECAT catalog.

2. Write a DLBL statement for an output file known to the program as IDLIST. Use a VSAM file named IDLIST.ERIE in the ERIECAT catalog.

3. Rewrite your above statement to retain the output file until the first day of 1988.

4. Now code a complete job using the above two data sets. The program's name is LISTIDS.

5. Change your job so that ERIECAT is a job catalog. Its file-ID is ERIE.CATALOG.TFILES.

6. Change your job to use a third file, known to the program as OPTIDS. Place OPTIDS in the VSAM data set OPTIONAL.PER-SONEL.IDS which is in the OPTCAT catalog.

✔ Answers to Chapter Exercise

1. ```
// DLBL NEWIDS,'TEMP.IDS.XMAS.ERIE',,VSAM,CAT=ERIECAT
```

2. ```
// DLBL IDLIST,'IDLIST.ERIE',,VSAM,CAT=ERIECAT
```

3. ```
// DLBL IDLIST,'IDLIST.ERIE',88/001,VSAM,CAT=ERIECAT
```

4. ```
// JOB CHAPEX
// DLBL NEWIDS,'TEMP.IDS.XMAS.ERIE',,VSAM,CAT=ERIECAT
// DLBL IDLIST,'IDLIST.ERIE',88/001,VSAM,CAT=ERIECAT
// EXEC LISTIDS,SIZE=AUTO
/&
```

5. ```
// JOB CHAPEX
// DLBL IJSYSUC,'ERIE.CATALOG.TFILES',,VSAM
// DLBL NEWIDS,'TEMP.IDS.XMAS.ERIE',,VSAM
// DLBL IDLIST,'IDLIST.ERIE',88/001,VSAM
// EXEC LISTIDS,SIZE=AUTO
/&
```

6. ```
// JOB CHAPEX
// DLBL IJSYSUC,'ERIE.CATALOG.TFILES',,VSAM
// DLBL NEWIDS,'TEMP.IDS.XMAS.ERIE',,VSAM
// DLBL IDLIST,'IDLIST.ERIE',88/001,VSAM
// DLBL OPTIDS,'OPTIONAL.PERSONEL.IDS',,VSAM,CAT=OPTCAT
// EXEC LISTIDS,SIZE=AUTO
/&
```

chapter five

JCL for Non-VSAM Files on Direct Access Devices

In the previous chapter, you learned how your JCL statements enable you to process files under the control of VSAM. In this chapter, you'll learn the statements necessary to process non-VSAM files on direct access devices.

At the end of this chapter, you'll be able to:

✔   Write an ASSGN statement for a DASD file

✔   Write an EXTENT statement for a DASD file

✔   Write a DLBL statement for a non-VSAM DASD file

✔   Write a complete job using non-VSAM DASD input and output files

Three Statements: ASSGN, DLBL, and EXTENT

At the time you define a VSAM file (using Access Methods
Services commands), all the information needed to access that
file is entered into a VSAM catalog. From that time on, VSAM
accesses your file by means of that catalog entry.

If you don't have the convenience of VSAM to manage your
files, you must provide the access information yourself. You do
this with three JCL statements: ASSGN, DLBL (Disk Label),
and EXTENT. The ASSGN statement for disk files associates a
file with a specific disk drive. DLBL provides label information.
The EXTENT statement specifies where on the disk the file is
located.

Here's a typical job using these statements to create a non-
VSAM file.

```
// JOB     SAMPLE
// ASSGN   SYS006,CKD,VOL=999999,SHR
// DLBL    TSTFILE,'TSTRECS'
// EXTENT  SYS006,999999,,,1244,50
// EXEC    TESTIT
/&
```

We'll discuss these statements in detail as we proceed
through this chapter, but for now we'll just say that the ASSGN
statement above assigns SYS006 in the source program to the
first available CKD device. It also specifies that volume 999999
is to be mounted on the chosen device. The DLBL statement
tells the system what to name the file ('TSTRECS'), and the
EXTENT statement tells where on the volume to put it, in this
case starting at track 1244 for a length of 50 tracks.

Let's take a closer look at each of these statements.

The ASSGN Statement

The format of the ASSGN statement for DASD devices is shown
at the top of the following page.

```
                            ⎛ address          ⎞
                            ⎜ (address-list)   ⎟
                            ⎜ type             ⎟
   // ASSGN SYSnnn,         ⎨ FBA              ⎬  [,VOL=nnnnnn][,SHR]
                            ⎜ CKD              ⎟
                            ⎜ DISK             ⎟
                            ⎜ DISKETTE         ⎟
                            ⎝ SYSnnn           ⎠
```

As with tape, be as general as possible whenever you can. DISK and DISKETTE are the most general designations. Figure 5.1 shows how the devices at an installation would be addressed. FBA and CKD are less general than DISK but more so than a type such as 3350. 3350 is more general than an address or address list.

Figure 5.1 Physical Unit Designations

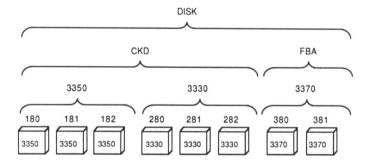

Here are some examples:

```
// ASSGN SYS006,DISK
```

This assigns the logical unit SYS006 to any disk device in the installation.

```
// ASSGN SYS006,CKD,VOL=942600
```

This assigns the logical unit SYS006 to any CKD device and specifies that volume 942600 be mounted on the chosen device. The SHR (share) parameter is important to system throughput. It lets your job access the same disk volume other jobs are using. It doesn't pertain to diskettes, which are never shared. Your job won't be held up waiting for exclusive control of the assigned volume, and other jobs won't be held up until you release the exclusive control (see Figure 5.2). Always code the SHR parameter for any disk device unless you're using a private volume.

Figure 5.2 The Effect of SHR

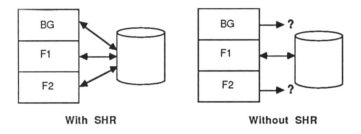

With SHR   Without SHR

```
// ASSGN SYS007,DISK,SHR
```

Here we request any available disk volume for SYS007.

```
// ASSGN SYS006,3350,VOL=450009,SHR
```

Here SYS006 is an input file on volume 450009. We request a 3350-type unit because that's what the volume requires. However, we also specify SHR because we don't care if other jobs use 450009 while it's mounted.

Your installation may have nonremovable FBA disks, in which case you may not need the ASSGN statement. Each disk could have its own, permanently assigned logical unit. For example, SYS006 might always refer to the disk at address 231, SYS007 might refer to the disk at 232, and so forth.

Check Your Understanding

1. Write a statement that temporarily assigns SYS009 to the first available CKD device. The volume you need has serial number 742001. (Don't forget to share.)

2. Write a statement to assign SYS010 to the 3350 device at address 232. Use the same volume as above.

3. Write the statement to assign SYS010 to the first available disk device. Any volume will do.

4. Write the statement to assign SYS010 to the first available 3350 device. Use volume number 999900.

5. What's wrong with this statement?

```
// ASSGN SYS006,DISKETTE,VOL=135260,SHR
```

✔ Answers

1. `// ASSGN SYS009,CKD,VOL=742001,SHR`

2. `// ASSGN SYS010,232,VOL=742001,SHR`

3. `// ASSGN SYS010,DISK,SHR`

4. `// ASSGN SYS010,3350,VOL=999900,SHR`

5. You can't share diskettes.

The DLBL Statement for Non-VSAM Files

DLBL's function is similar to TLBL's. DLBL contains file label information for DASD label checking and label creation processes, and it enables your program to connect and disconnect the file you specify. Figure 5.3 shows the format of a disk label and Figure 5.4 shows the format of a diskette label.

Figure 5.3 Format 1 Disk Label

Columns	Contents
1–44	File-ID
45	Label format identifier
46–51	File serial number
52–53	Volume sequence number
54–56	Creation date
57–59	Expiration date
60	Extent count
61–62	Not used in VSE
63–75	System code (IBMDOSVS)
76–78	Date last accessed
79–80	Not used
81–82	FBA control interval size
83–84	File organization
85	Not used
86–93	Used only with ISAM
94	Last volume/DSF indicators
95	Original request indicator
96–103	Not used in VSE
104–105	Negative displacement
106–115	First extent
106	Extent type
107	Extent sequence number
108–111	Lower limit
112–115	Upper limit
116–125	Second extent
116	Extent type
117	Extent sequence number
118–121	Lower limit
122–125	Upper limit
126–135	Third extent
126	Extent type
127	Extent sequence number
128–131	Lower limit
132–135	Upper limit
136–140	Pointer to next label (if more extents)

Figure 5.4 Diskette Label

Columns	Contents
1–4	Label identifier (HDR1)
5	Not used
6–13	File-ID
14–22	Not used
23–27	Record length
28	Not used
29–33	Beginning of extent
34	Not used
35–39	End of extent
40	Not used
41	Bypass indicator
42	File security indicator
43	Write-protection indicator
44	Must be blank
45	Multivolume indicator
46–47	Volume sequence number
48–53	Creation date
54–66	Not used
67–72	Expiration date
73	Verify indicator
74	Not used
75–79	End-of-data address
80	Not used

Here are the formats of the DLBL statement for non-VSAM files. You'll notice they're similar to the VSAM DLBL, but they have some different operands.

For disk:

```
// DLBL filename,['file-ID'],[date],[code][,DSF]
      ┌,BLKSIZE=n┐
      │,CISIZE=n │
      └          ┘
```

For diskette:

```
// DLBL filename,['file-ID'],[date],DU
```

The first four operands are positional operands, and they must appear in this order if you use them. Remember to substitute a comma for any positional operand you do not use unless there are no more positional operands following. Operands from DSF through CISIZE may appear in any order, and they may be omitted without substituting a comma.

As with TLBL, the filename is the program's name for the file.

The file-ID is the file's actual name as it appears in the label entry. For disk files this can be up to 44 characters. Diskette files are limited to eight characters for the file-ID.

The date gives an expiration date or a retention period for an output file. Use the nnnn format to specify a retention period or yy/ddd for an expiration date. The date in DLBL affects only output files, in contrast to the date in a TLBL statement. If you specify a date on an input TLBL, VSE checks the file's *creation* date and notifies the operator if it doesn't match. But that doesn't happen with DLBL. VSE ignores the date on an input file's DLBL.

The code field indicates the type of file. The codes you will use are:

SD   sequential disk file (SAM)

DU   diskette file (SAM)

VSAM   for all files controlled by VSAM

You used VSAM in the last chapter. This chapter is concerned with SD and DU. If you omit the code, the system assumes you want SD.

The DSF operand means that a Data Secured File is to be created or processed. As a security measure, the operator is notified by a console message if any data secured file is accessed. This helps to prevent unauthorized access to sensitive data, but frankly, it's not enough. If your installation is concerned about data security, it has probably added a security package that does a better job than "vanilla" VSE. (ICCF's security system is sufficient for many installations.) If you need to work with sensitive data, find out about your installation's data security system. DSF is not used for diskettes.

BLKSIZE (blocksize) and CISIZE (control interval size) control how data records are blocked in a SAM file. A DLBL statement can contain one or the other, but not both. BLKSIZE pertains to SAM files on CKD devices and CISIZE to SAM files on FBA devices. CISIZE must be a multiple of 512, the FBA block size.

Your program already specifies or implies the block or control interval size. Why override it? For an input file, override it only if the value in the program is wrong. If the actual block or control interval size on the file is different from what the program says, use BLKSIZE or CISIZE to specify the correct values. How could this happen? Maybe the job that creates the input file was modified. Or maybe you're using the program on a different input file than it was intended for. VSE JCL gives you the flexibility to handle this without changing your program.

For an output file, you might want to change the block or control interval size. A larger size makes your program run faster and saves disk space but takes up more memory space during execution. A smaller size decreases memory usage but makes your program run longer and uses more disk space. If you're not sure how to make your program more efficient, check with your friendly local systems programmer. And don't forget that changing the block size here means you must modify any job that accesses the file.

BLKSIZE and CISIZE are not used with diskette files.

✓ Check Your Understanding

Code DLBL statements for these sequential, non-VSAM files.

1. Your program calls an input file INRECORD. Its real name is CASHFLOW.FORECAST.585. It's a sequential file on disk.

2. Your program calls an output file REJECTS. Put it on diskette and call it REJRECS. Retain it at least 30 days.

3. Your program calls an output file NEWFILE. Put it on disk (CKD) and call it LOCAL.MAILLIST. Retain it 90 days. Override the program's blocking and establish a block size of 2048 bytes.

4. Change your answer to item 3 to put the file on an FBA device. Also request VSE's data security facility for the file.

5. What's wrong with these statements?

   a. `// ASSGN SYS006,FBA`
      `// DLBL INFILE,'NEWRECS',,SD,BLKSIZE=3000`

   b. `// ASSGN SYS006,DISKETTE`
      `// DLBL INFILE,'LOSSDATA',DSF`

   c. `// DLBL INFILE,'LOSSDATA',DU`

   e. `// DLBL OUTFILE,'NEWDISK',BLKSIZE=1024,CISIZE=4096`

   d. `// DLBL OUTFILE,'JULY.REPORT',,DU`

   f. `// DLBL OUTFILE,'JULY.REPORT',CISIZE=4000`

✔ Answers

1. `// DLBL INRECORD,'CASHFLOW.FORECAST.585',,SD`

   You could have omitted the last operand and the preceding two commas since SD is the default.

2. `// DLBL REJECTS,'REJRECS',30,DU`

3. `// DLBL NEWFILE,'LOCAL.MAILLIST',90,SD,BLKSIZE=2048`

   You could have omitted SD and its comma.

4. `// DLBL NEWFILE,'LOCAL.MAILLIST',90,SD,DSF,CISIZE=2048`

   You could have omitted SD and its comma. DSF and CISIZE could be reversed.

5. a. You can't use BLKSIZE with FBA.
   b. With diskette, the DLBL must specify DU and can't specify DSF.
   c. DU must be in the fourth position, not third.
   d. You can't use both BLKSIZE and CISIZE in the same DLBL; one pertains to CKD and one to FBA.
   e. Diskette file-ID's are limited to eight characters.
   f. CISIZE must be a multiple of 512.

The EXTENT Statement

One wonderful feature of VSAM is that it decides where to place files on a disk. When you're not using VSAM, you must do this yourself. Some installations include a disk management utility that handles assigning space to files. Your systems programmer can let you know if this is true for you.

Figure 5.5 shows what a disk's storage space may look like after it's been used awhile. Because many files have been created, extended, and deleted, the available space is broken up into small chunks all over the disk. VSE may have to segment your file to fit it on the disk.

Figure 5.5 File Extents

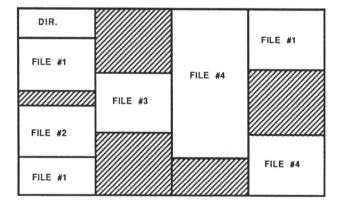

Each area of continuous space used by a file is known as an *extent*. Seven extents appear in Figure 5.5; file #1 has three extents and file #4 has two.

Now suppose you must add to the disk file #5, which is the same size as file #4's first extent. Where can you put it? Try to use as few extents as possible, because each additional extent slows processing of the file. Figure 5.6, on the next page, shows our solution. We had to use three extents.

Figure 5.6 Adding File Extents

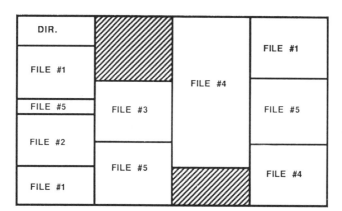

You can find out the available space on a volume by listing its VTOC (volume table of contents).

EXTENT statements identify where a file is on disk. They are required for all non-VSAM DASD output files. They are not required for input files since the disk directory points to each file's extents. They *are* required for input files spread over more than one volume, however, as the directory doesn't indicate additional volumes. A file's EXTENT statements must immediately follow its DLBL statement.

Let's look at a sample job that creates file #5 in Figure 5.6.

```
// JOB MAKEFILE
// ASSGN SYS006,DISK,VOL=300561,SHR
// ASSGN SYS007,DISK,VOL=300561,SHR
// DLBL INFILE,'JUNE.INVENTORY.DATA'
// DLBL OUTFILE,'JUNE.BACKORDERS',30
// EXTENT SYS007,300561,,1,316,100
// EXTENT ,,,2,714,300
// EXTENT ,,,3,1065,300
// EXEC BACKORDS
/&
```

The file on SYS006 requires no EXTENT statement because it is used as input. The output file on SYS007 requires three EXTENT statements immediately following its DLBL. Each statement identifies one extent. The first extent starts at track

316 and extends for 100 tracks. The second starts at track 714 for 300 tracks; the third starts at track 1065 for 300 tracks. These tracks (or blocks on an FBA device) are now reserved for JUNE.BACKORDERS, whether or not the current job records data on them. This job may fill only the first 400 tracks, but the remaining 300 tracks have been allocated to the file and can't be used by any other file.

Now let's look at the format of the EXTENT statement for disk files (not diskettes):

```
// EXTENT [symbolic-unit],[serial-no.],[type],[sequence-no.],
         [starting track or block],[no. of tracks or blocks]
```

Every operand is positional, so you'll need to use commas to indicate omissions. The following sections give details about each of these operands.

Symbolic-Unit Operand

This six-character field in the format SYSxxx matches the logical-unit operand of your ASSGN statement so that the system can connect the extent to the device named in the program.

If you omit the symbolic-unit operand, the symbolic unit of the preceding EXTENT statement is used. If the symbolic unit is omitted from the first EXTENT statement, the system uses the logical unit named in the program. If that's OK with you, this first EXTENT operand could be omitted. But we suggest including it on the first EXTENT statement for each file.

Serial-Number Operand

This is the serial number of the volume containing the extent, and it matches the VOL=operand of the ASSGN statement.

Recall that with tapes and VSAM you often let the system select the volume by not specifying the volume serial number. But when you're assigning extents, you must know what volume you're working with and make sure to specify that volume in your ASSGN and EXTENT statements. So a non-VSAM DASD output file is defined like this:

```
// ASSGN SYS007,DISK,VOL=457965,SHR
// DLBL OUTFILE,'TESTRUN.OUTRECS'
// EXTENT SYS007,457965,...
```

Notice that both the ASSGN statement and the EXTENT statement specify unit SYS007 and volume 457965.

If you omit the serial number, VSE picks up the serial number from the preceding EXTENT statement.

We usually omit the symbolic unit and the serial number from the second and following EXTENT statements for a file. We put them on the first EXTENT statement only. That way, if they change, we have to change only one statement.

Extent-Type Operand

This operand is a one-digit code indicating the type of extent. The only type you'll use is 1, which indicates a normal data area. Since that's the default, you can always omit this operand if you like, being sure to code the comma.

Sequence-Number Operand

If your file has several extents on the same volume, the sequence number gives the position of this extent, from 0 to 255. If you omit this operand, the extents are used in the order of the EXTENT statements. The example given earlier uses 1, 2, and 3 for this operand in the three EXTENT statements.

Starting Track/Block Operand

This operand gives the beginning location (relative track or block number) of the extent. If you're using a CKD device, this operand gives the track number relative to zero (the first track). If you're using an FBA device, this operand supplies the block number.

Example:

```
// DLBL NEWTIMES,'TV.LISTINGS.923',30
// EXTENT SYS002,403001,,,1925 (remaining operands.....)
```

Here we've specified a beginning location of block number 1925. The extra commas indicate we've omitted the code and sequence number operands, so that 1 will be used for each of those values.

Number of Tracks/Blocks Operand

This operand gives the number of CKD tracks or FBA blocks to be included in the extent. Be accurate in your estimate; over-estimating wastes valuable disk space; underestimating can cause your program to bomb. For CKD devices, specify from one to five digits to give the number of tracks required.

For FBA devices, specify anywhere from 1 to 2,147,483,645 blocks (each block is 512 bytes). Make the extent size a multiple of the CISIZE. For example, if the CISIZE is eight blocks (4096 bytes), the extent size should be a multiple of eight, such as 400 blocks. Figure 5.7 shows what happens if you don't use a multiple of the CISIZE. Here, the CISIZE is eight blocks and the extent size is 404 blocks. The last four blocks in the extent can never be used since they don't fit in a control interval.

Figure 5.7 Wasted Blocks in an Extent

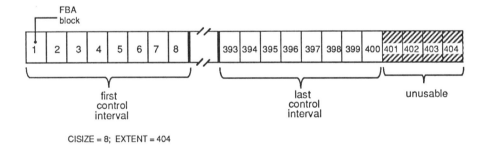

CISIZE = 8; EXTENT = 404

Example:

```
// DLBL NEWTIMES,'TV.LISTINGS.923',30
// EXTENT SYS002,43001,,,1925,580
```

Now we've added to our example the fact that we need 580 blocks. The last two operands, starting position and length, fully define the location of the extent.

Check Your Understanding

1. Write an EXTENT statement for an output file (SYS007) on CKD volume 456900. Start the file on track 49 and give it 200 tracks.

2. Write an EXTENT statement for an output file (SYS007) on FBA volume 111000. Start the file at block 1000 and give it 60 blocks.

3. Write EXTENT statements for a file (SYS007) to be put on FBA volume 101010. It needs three extents:
   a. Start at block 400, continue for 200 blocks.
   b. Start at block 1500, continue for 200 blocks.
   c. Start at block 2000, continue for 300 blocks.

4. Which of these files need EXTENT statements?
   a. An input file using three extents on a CKD device.
   b. An input file using one extent on an FBA device.
   c. An output file needing two extents on an FBA device.
   d. An output file needing one extent on a diskette.

5. What's wrong with these statements?
   a. ```
      // DLBL OUTFILE,'NEWRECS',CISIZE=5120
      // EXTENT SYS007,123456,,,,200,99
      ```

   b. ```
      // ASSGN SYS110,CKD,VOL=444000,SHR
      // DLBL OUTFILE,'INVENTRY.CONTROL.DATA'
      // EXTENT SYS110,444555,,,200,99
      ```

✔ **Answers**

1. ```
   // EXTENT SYS007,456900,,,,49,200
   ```

2. ```
   // EXTENT SYS007,111000,,,,1000,60
   ```

3. ```
   // EXTENT SYS007,101010,,1,400,200
   // EXTENT ,,,2,1500,200
   // EXTENT ,,,3,2000,300
   ```
   ```

You could omit the sequence numbers as long as you put the statements in this order. You might have included the symbolic unit and the volume serial number on any or all statements.

4. c, d

5. a. The extent size of 99 blocks is not a multiple of the CISIZE (10 blocks); nine blocks will be wasted in this extent.
   b. The volume numbers on the ASSGN statement and the EXTENT statement don't match. (Later extents might be on different volumes but the first one should be on the assigned volume.)

Diskette Files

Diskette files are easier to write EXTENT statements for. A file can have only one extent per diskette, and VSE decides where to put it. All you need provide is the first two parameters. Even so, the EXTENT statement is required for output files.

```
// ASSGN SYS007,DISKETTE,VOL=222111
// DLBL DISKOUT,'ACCTREC',90,DU
// EXTENT SYS007,222111
```

It seems a bit redundant that the same information appears in the ASSGN statement, but that's the way VSE expects to receive the information.

Input Files

EXTENT statements are never required for input files (unless more than one volume is involved). All the necessary informa tion is in the file's label entry. But if you do provide it, VSE checks it and notifies the operator if it doesn't match. Most programmers don't think this extra check is necessary (or even wise), and they don't include EXTENT statements for input files.

✓ Check Your Understanding

Now you can write complete jobs involving disk files.

1. Write a job to use these two files:

Input	Output
SYS006	SYS007 (no assignment
diskette volume 129000	necessary)
logical name: LANDRECS	FBA volume 333333; start at
real name: LANDRECS	block 1250 for 50 blocks
	logical name: FILLOUT
	real name: LANDFILL.DATA
	Save for 60 days

Execute the program named LANDFILL.

2. Write a job to execute the program named NEWHIRES.

Input	Output
unit record	SYS007
	CKD volume 123456; two
	extents

start	length
301	100 tracks
517	100 tracks

logical name: NEWNAMES
real name:
    NEWHIRE.DATA.AUG

✔ Answers

```
1. // JOB LANDJOB
   // ASSGN SYS006,DISKETTE,VOL=129000
   // DLBL LANDRECS,'LANDRECS',,DU
   // DLBL FILLOUT,'LANDFILL.DATA',60
   // EXTENT SYS007,333333,,,1250,50
   // EXEC LANDFILL
   /&
```

```
2. // JOB HIRING
   // ASSGN SYS007,CKD,VOL=123456,SHR
   // DLBL NEWNAMES,'NEWHIRE.DATA.AUG'
   // EXTENT SYS007,123456,,,301,100
   // EXTENT ,,,,517,100
   // EXEC NEWHIRES
      (input records go here)
   /*
   /&
```

Chapter Summary

In this chapter you've learned to use the ASSGN, EXTENT, and DLBL statements to access data on direct access devices when VSAM is not available.

You've learned to code the operands of these statements to fit CKD, FBA, or diskette devices. You've also learned to access files that exist in multiple extents on one volume.

You'll find a reference chart summarizing the various statements and operands for both VSAM and non-VSAM files in Appendix A.

✓ Chapter Exercise

Now you should be able to pull together what you've learned about unit record files, VSAM, and non-VSAM files by coding some complete jobs.

1. Code a job to execute program UPDATE. As input, use VSAM data set CLAIMS.1984; the program calls it MASTER. Output will be: (a) a VSAM data set (NEWMAST) called ANNUAL.RE-PORT and (b) a tape file (SYS008) to be called CLAIMS.UP-DATE. Assign it to any available tape device and volume. Retain output for 30 days. Both VSAM data sets are controlled by the ACCAT catalog.

2. Code a job using tape input (SYS007) on any tape drive. The file-ID is SCHEDULE. Mount tape volume 146290. Output is a printed report. Use the standard assignment for the printer. Execute program PRINTIT.

3. Code a job using a tape file (SYS008) as input. The file-ID is TESTFILE; the program calls it TESTOUT. Use volume serial number 740026, on any available tape drive. Output goes to two non-VSAM SAM files on CKD:

SYS010   on volume 860001 in one extent, starting at track 650 for 80 tracks. Filename is TST1, and file-ID is TEST1.

SYS011   on volume 860051 in 2 extents (one at track 740 for 20 tracks and one at track 800 for 100 tracks). Filename is TST2, and file-ID is TEST2.

Retain output for 7 days. Files are not data secured. Execute program TESTIT.

4. Code a job using two VSAM data sets as input.

Filename: MERGE1   **File-ID:** PERSONEL.FULLTIME.CHICAGO

MERGE2   PERSONEL.PARTTIME.CHICAGO

These files are in the existing CHIPERS catalog. Execute program MERGER.

Have one tape (SYS008) as output on any available tape device. Filename is MERGEOUT and file-ID is PERSONEL. ALL.CHI. Retain output until the last day of 1999.

✔ Answers to Chapter Exercise

```
1. // JOB CLAIMJOB
   // ASSGN SYS008,TAPE
   // DLBL MASTER,'CLAIMS.1984',,VSAM,CAT=ACCAT
   // TLBL SYS008,'CLAIMS.UPDATES',30
   // DLBL NEWMAST,'ANNUAL.REPORT',30,VSAM,CAT=ACCAT
   // EXEC UPDATE,SIZE=AUTO
   /&

2. // JOB SCHEDJOB
   // ASSGN SYS007,TAPE,VOL=146290
   // TLBL SYS007,'SCHEDULE'
   // EXEC PRINTIT
   /&

3. // JOB TESTJOB
   // ASSGN SYS008,TAPE,VOL=740026
   // ASSGN SYS010,CKD,VOL=860001,SHR
   // ASSGN SYS011,CKD,VOL=860051,SHR
   // TLBL TESTOUT,'TESTFILE'
   // DLBL TST1,'TEST1'
   // EXTENT SYS010,860001,,,650,80
   // DLBL TST2,'TEST2'
   // EXTENT SYS011,860051,,,740,20
   // EXTENT ,,,,800,100
   // EXEC TESTIT
   /&
```

```
4. // JOB MERGEJOB
   // ASSGN SYS008,TAPE
   // TLBL MERGOUT,'PERSONNEL.ALL.CHI',99/365
   // DLBL MERGE1,'PERSONNEL.FULLTIME.CHICAGO',,VSAM,CAT=CHIPERS
   // DLBL MERGE2,'PERSONNEL.PARTTIME.CHICAGO',,VSAM,CAT=CHIPERS
   // EXEC MERGER,SIZE=AUTO
   /&
```

Using Private Libraries

You've already learned about the four types of VSE libraries (Source Statement, Relocatable, Core Image, and Procedure) and how your jobs interact with them. You might want to review Figure 1.5 before starting this chapter. All the jobs you've written so far have used the system libraries by default. This chapter shows you how to use private libraries.

When you have completed this chapter, you'll be able to:

✔ Write ASSGN and DLBL statements to access a private library

✔ Write a LIBDEF statement to establish a library search chain

✔ Write a complete job that uses private libraries

Systems vs. Private Libraries

The only required library in VSE is the system Core Image Library. However, your installation probably has all four system libraries. In addition, many private libraries of all four types are probably in use. Private libraries add security and help take the burden off the system libraries.

When your job does not request any private libraries, VSE assumes you want to use the system libraries. For example, look at this job:

```
// JOB  LISTLINE
// EXEC LISTER
   (input records)
/*
/&
```

Where will VSE look for the program named LISTER? In the system Core Image Library.

Suppose LISTER is not in the system library but in a private Core Image Library named TESTLIB. The job to execute LISTER might look like this:

```
// JOB LISTLINE
// LIBDEF CL,SEARCH=TESTLIB
// EXEC LISTER
   (input records)
/*
/&
```

The LIBDEF (Library Definition) statement tells VSE to search the Core Image Library (CL) named TESTLIB for the phases executed in this job.

The ASSGN and DLBL statements can also be used to access private libraries in limited cases. Here's an example:

```
// JOB COMPJOB
// ASSGN SYSSLB,DISK,VOL=347295,SHR
// DLBL IJSYSSL,'PERS.DEPT.SSL'
// EXEC PROC=COBCOMP
   (unit record input here)
/*
/&
```

This compile job uses a private Source Statement Library named PERS.DEPT.SSL. Its symbolic unit is SYSSLB and the compiler program calls it IJSYSSL.

First we'll show you how to use ASSGN and DLBL to access a private library. Then we'll show you how to use LIBDEF, which is much more flexible and comprehensive.

Using ASSGN and DLBL

When you assign a private library to a job, the system accesses the assigned library first to find the elements your program needs. If the system doesn't find the elements in the private library, it automatically searches the system library next.

Some limitations exist: (1) you can't assign system libraries; (2) you can't assign private Procedure or Core Image Libraries; (3) only one private Source Statement or one Relocatable Library can be assigned to a job at any given time. Therefore, the only time you would use ASSGN and DLBL to specify a private library is when you're compiling (or assembling) and link editing, as those are the only times the Source Statement and Relocatable Libraries are used.

You use special logical units for the ASSGN statement and special filenames for the DLBL statement:

Source Statement Library:
      logical unit   SYSSLB
      filename   IJSYSSL

Relocatable Library:
      logical unit   SYSRLB
      filename   IJSYSRL

Here's another example:

```
// JOB LINKJOB
// ASSGN SYSRLB,DISK,VOL=459999,SHR
// DLBL IJSYSRL,'PRIV.RELO.PAYDAY'
// EXEC PROC=COBLINK
```

These statements assign a private Relocatable Library for a link editing step. The ASSGN statement uses the logical unit SYSRLB, and the DLBL statement uses the name IJSYSRL. That's how VSE knows a private Relocatable Library is being assigned.

Figure 6.1 illustrates the library setup for this job. The cataloged procedure COBLINK, located in the *system* Procedure Library, invokes the linkage editor, located in the *system* Core Image Library. When the linkage editor accesses an object module, VSE looks first in the private library named PRIV.RE-LO.PAYDAY, then in the system library.

Figure 6.1 Using a Private Relocatable Library

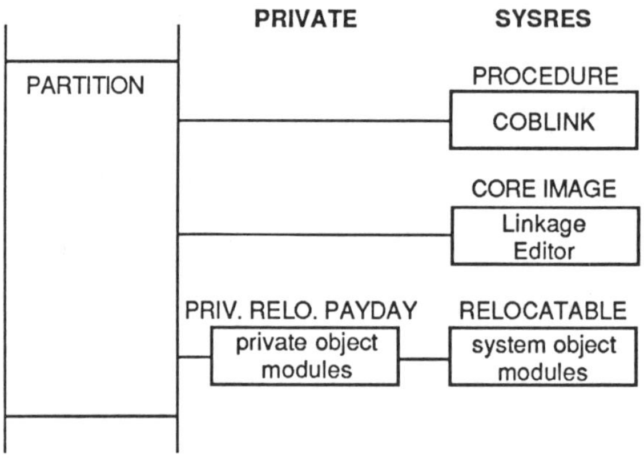

✓ Check Your Understanding

1. Suppose you're working on a new accounts receivable system for your company. All source modules are kept in a private Source Statement Library called BILLING.TEST.SSL. All object modules are kept in a private Relocatable Library called BILLING.TEST.RL. Both libraries are on volume 440000.

   Now you want to compile a source program. Use the cataloged procedure called COBCOMP, which invokes the COBOL compiler and catalogs the output in the Relocatable Library.

   a. Write a job that calls COBCOMP using BILLING.TEST.SSL and BILLING.TEST.RL. Your job needs a unit record input file (your source program).

b. Whenever your source program says COPY, where will VSE look first for the book to be copied?

c. Where will the compiler's output (the object module) be stored?

2. a. Now you want to link edit your new object module. Write a job to do so. Use the cataloged procedure COBLINK. You'll need a unit record input file.

b. Where will VSE look first for your object module?

✔ Answers

1. a.
```
// JOB COMPJOB
// ASSGN SYSSLB,DISK,VOL=440000,SHR
// ASSGN SYSRLB,DISK,VOL=440000,SHR
// DLBL IJSYSSL,'BILLING.TEST.SSL'
// DLBL IJSYSRL,'BILLING.TEST.RL'
// EXEC PROC=COBCOMP
   (unit record input here)
/*
/&
```

b. BILLING.TEST.SSL

c. BILLING.TEST.RL

2. a.
```
// JOB LINKJOB
// ASSGN SYSRLB,DISK,VOL=440000,SHR
// DLBL IJSYSRL,'BILLING.TEST.RL'
// EXEC PROC=COBLINK
   (unit record input here)
/*
/&
```

b. BILLING.TEST.RL

THE LIBDEF Statement

ASSGN and DLBL have many limitations when used with private libraries. LIBDEF is much more useful. With LIBDEF you can: (1) assign all four types of libraries; (2) assign multiple libraries of each type; and (3) specify the order in which the libraries are searched, including the system libraries. LIBDEF establishes a temporary or permanent chain of libraries in the sequence you want them searched.

Figure 6.2 shows how you can set up libraries using LIBDEF. In the example, the first partition has eight defined chains: one permanent and one temporary for each type of library. This is the maximum number of chains.

Figure 6.2 Sample Library Chains

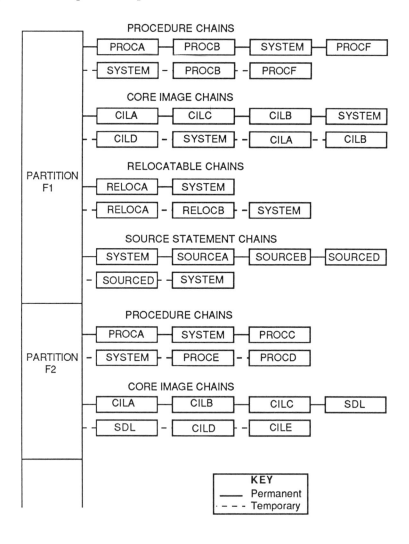

Temporary chains are established by a job for the purpose of that job only. They are automatically dropped when the job terminates. Usually they include only the libraries needed by that job, in the order of most frequent access so that search times are minimized. For example, look at the temporary chains established for the job running in the first partition in Figure 6.2. We can assume that: (1) this is a huge job since so many libraries are accessed (at least three procedures and at least four programs); (2) the job includes compilation or the Source Statement Libraries wouldn't be needed; (3) most of the source modules to be compiled are in SOURCED, since it's first in the chain; (4) most of the procedures to be used are in the system Procedure Library, etc.

Permanent chains are associated with the partition and apply to all jobs using that partition. When a partition has permanent chains and a job specifies temporary chains, VSE searches the temporary chain first. Then, if the desired element has not been found, VSE searches the permanent chain. Finally, the system library is searched, if it wasn't included in a chain. Refer to the Source Statement Library chains attached to partition F1 in Figure 6.2. Suppose the job occupying the partition calls for a book located in SOURCEB. Will VSE find it? Eventually, yes. But first VSE will look in SOURCED, the system library, the system library again, and SOURCEA. That's bad programming practice. SOURCEB should be included in the temporary chain if the job needs it.

Core Image Library chains are handled slightly differently. A System Directory List (SDL) automatically becomes the first member of the chain. The SDL contains the locations of frequently used phases, such as the COBOL compiler, to help speed access.

If the phase is not found in the SDL, the name of the phase itself determines the next library to be searched. If the phase name begins with a "$", the search sequence is:

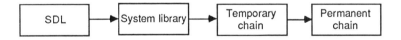

If the phase name does not begin with a "$", the search sequence is:

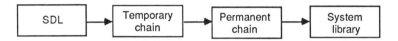

When you're naming a phase, avoid using $ as the first character. Put your phases in private libraries and leave the system Core Image Library free for IBM-provided transient phases that do system work.

☑ Check Your Understanding

1. How many search chains can you establish per partition using LIBDEF statements?

2. If a partition has both a temporary and a permanent Source Statement chain, which chain is searched first?

3. If the book is not found in the temporary or permanent search chain, VSE automatically searches the _____ library.

4. What element speeds access to phases in the Core Image Library by listing the location of frequently used phases?

5. Indicate the search order for phases.

_____ a. If the phasename begins with a $

_____ b. If the phasename does not begin with a $

1. SDL, temporary chain, permanent chain, system library

2. System library, permanent chain, temporary chain, SDL

3. SDL, system library, temporary chain, permanent chain

✔ Answers

1. Eight: one temporary and one permanent of each type

2. Temporary

3. System

4. SDL (System Directory List)

5. a. 3
   b. 1

How to Use the LIBDEF Statement

Suppose you've established several private Source Statement Libraries containing books you use often in your programs. Your newest program needs books from your BILLSSL, PERSSL, and INVSSL libraries. By placing a LIBDEF statement at the beginning of your job following the JOB statement, you can tell the system that you will be accessing Source Statement Libraries, and that you want the system to search BILLSSL, PERSSL, and INVSSL to find the books you need. Let's say the majority of the books are in BILLSSL. Most of the rest are in PERSSL. Only one book is in INVSSL. Your LIBDEF statement would look like this:

```
// LIBDEF SL,SEARCH=(BILLSSL,PERSSL,INVSSL)
```

The first operand tells the system the type of library you want to access. Your choices are:

CL   for Core Image Library

RL   for Relocatable Library

SL   for Source Statement Library

PL   for Procedure Library

The SEARCH operand lets you state the actual names of the libraries to be searched and the sequence in which you want them searched. The search list is enclosed in parentheses. Follow these rules in forming the SEARCH operand:

1. Each library name may be one to seven characters in length, and it must be the same as the filename on the DLBL statement identifying the library. You probably won't need to include the DLBL statement for the job. It's probably permanently stored in VSE's label information area.

2. To include the system library in the chain, use the name IJSYSRS. IJSYSRS is used for all four types of system library. If you don't specify IJSYSRS, it is automatically included in its default position: first for phases starting with $; last for all other phases and all other types of libraries.

3. For temporary Core Image chains, you can move the System Directory List (SDL) from its default position to another point in the chain by using the name SDL.

4. SDL must always come before IJSYSRS in a CL search chain.

5. You can't use SDL in a permanent chain.

The system assumes that your search chain is temporary unless you specify otherwise by adding the operand "PERM" like this:

```
// LIBDEF SL,SEARCH=(BILLSSL,PERSSL,INVSSL),PERM
```

Most installations don't want you to change the permanent chains, so you'll probably define only temporary chains.

Here's the format of the LIBDEF statement:

$$// \text{ LIBDEF } \begin{Bmatrix} \text{CL} \\ \text{RL} \\ \text{SL} \\ \text{PL} \end{Bmatrix}, \text{SEARCH}=(\text{name,name}\ldots) \begin{bmatrix} ,\text{TEMP} \\ ,\text{PERM} \end{bmatrix}$$

We've omitted some parameters that don't pertain to defining search chains. You'll learn some of them later.

Check Your Understanding

1. Write a LIBDEF statement to establish a temporary search chain for Source Statement Libraries MINE, YOURS, and OURS, in that order.

2. Rewrite the statement in the question above, moving the system library to the second position in the search chain.

3. Write a LIBDEF statement to establish a temporary search chain for Core Image Libraries ABC, XYZ, and 123, in that order.

4. Rewrite the statement in question 3 above so that the System Directory List is in the third search position.

5. What's wrong with these statements?
   a. `// LIBDEF CL,SEARCH=(IJSYSRS,LIBX,SDL)`

   b. `// LIBDEF CL,SEARCH=(CORE9,CORE8,CORE3,SDL),PERM`

   c. `// LIBDEF PL,SEARCH=(PROC1,SDL,PROC2,IJSYSRS)`

✔ **Answers**

1. `// LIBDEF SL,SEARCH=(MINE,YOURS,OURS)`

2. `// LIBDEF SL,SEARCH=(MINE,IJSYSRS,YOURS,OURS)`

3. `// LIBDEF CL,SEARCH=(ABC,XYZ,123)`

4. `// LIBDEF CL,SEARCH=(ABC,XYZ,SDL,123)`

5. a. SDL must come before IJSYSRS
   b. Can't use SDL with a permanent chain
   c. SDL is used only with Core Image Libraries

Chapter Summary

This chapter has shown you how to use private libraries in a job. You can assign one private Source Statement Library or one private Relocatable Library using ASSGN and DLBL. Use SYSSLB and SYSRLB as the logical units and IJSYSSL and IJSYSRL as the filenames. Other than that, these statements are handled just as they are for other files.

The LIBDEF statement establishes a chain of libraries to be searched. Your installation probably has established all the appropriate permanent chains for each partition. You can speed your job by specifying temporary chains, which are automatically dropped when your job ends. Except for Core Image Libraries, VSE's search order is temporary chain, permanent chain, system library (if not included in the temporary or permanent chain). For Core Image Libraries, for phases starting with $, the search order is SDL (if not included in the temporary or permanent chain), system library (if not included in the temporary or permanent chain), temporary chain, permanent chain. For phases beginning with a character other than $, the search order is SDL (if not included in the temporary or permanent chain), temporary chain, permanent chain, system library (if not included in the temporary or permanent chain). You include the SDL in a chain by using the filename SDL; you probably shouldn't do this, as it defeats the purpose of the SDL. You include the system library (any type) by using the filename IJSYSRS.

$$
\texttt{// LIBDEF} \begin{Bmatrix} \texttt{CL} \\ \texttt{RL} \\ \texttt{SL} \\ \texttt{PL} \end{Bmatrix} \texttt{,SEARCH=(name,name...)} \begin{bmatrix} \texttt{,TEMP} \\ \texttt{,PERM} \end{bmatrix}
$$

✓ Chapter Exercise

1. Write ASSGN and DLBL statements that access a private Relocatable Library named SECTION5.PRL.

2. Write ASSGN and DLBL statements that access a private Source Statement Library named PROJSTAR.PSSL. (Volume 123000.)

3. Write a LIBDEF statement to establish a temporary chain of private Core Image Libraries in this order: BUYCIL, SELLCIL, XCHGCIL. Let the SDL and the system library fall in their default positions.

4. Rewrite your preceding statement so the system library is searched first (after the SDL), regardless of the phase name.

5. Rewrite your preceding statement so the SDL and the system library are always searched after BUYCIL, SELLCIL, and XCHGCIL.

6. Now write a complete job to execute a cataloged procedure named COBGO. This job compiles, link edits, and places a phase in the Core Image Library, then executes that phase. All four types of libraries are involved, and you want to use four private libraries, named MYSSL, MYRL, MYPL, and MYCIL. Any elements not found in these libraries will be found in the system libraries; no other private libraries are involved. Don't worry about any other files for this job; it would need some input and output files defined, but we want you to concentrate on the libraries in this exercise.

✔ Answers to Chapter Exercise

```
1. // ASSGN  SYSRLB,DISK,VOL=123000,SHR
   // DLBL   IJSYSRL,'SECTION5.PRL'

2. // ASSGN  SYSSLB,DISK,VOL=123000,SHR
   // DLBL   IJSYSSL,'PROJSTAR.PSSL'

3. // LIBDEF CL,SEARCH=(BUYCIL,SELLCIL,XCHGCIL)

4. // LIBDEF CL,SEARCH=(IJSYSRS,BUYCIL,SELLCIL,XCHGCIL)

5. // LIBDEF CL,SEARCH=(BUYCIL,SELLCIL,XCHGCIL,SDL,IJSYSRS)
```

```
6. // JOB   TESTPROG
   // LIBDEF SL,SEARCH=(MYSSL,IJSYSRS)
   // LIEDEF RL,SEARCH=(MYRL,IJSYSRS)
   // LIBDEF PL,SEARCH=(MYPL,IJSYSRS)
   // LIBDEF CL,SEARCH=(MYCIL,IJSYSRS)
   // EXEC PROC=COBGO
   // &
```

We included IJSYSRS in each chain so it would be searched before the permanent chain.

Creating and Using Cataloged Procedures

You've seen in previous chapters that jobs may consist of a great many JCL statements, some of which are quite involved. If one of these complex or lengthy jobs happens to be a job you use often, it would be tedious to rekey the job each time you want to use it.

Luckily, DOS/VSE saves you from this kind of misery by letting you create *cataloged procedures* (sets of JCL statements) that you can execute with just one command.

This chapter will show you how to create a procedure and how to use it. At the end of the chapter, you'll be able to:

✔ Write a job to catalog a procedure to the Procedure Library

✔ Write a job to invoke a cataloged procedure

✔ Add, change, and delete statements in an existing procedure

✔ Write jobs to list the directory and contents of the Procedure Library

✔ Use private Procedure Libraries

A Sample Case

Imagine that you must execute this job every day:

```
// JOB GETREPT
// DLBL IJSYSUC,'DEPT.USER.CAT',,VSAM
// DLBL SYS220,'INVENTORY.MASTER',,VSAM
// DLBL SYS240,'WAREHOUS.ORDERS',,VSAM
// DLBL SYS250,'BACK.ORDERS',,VSAM
// DLBL USER2,'USER.CAT.WAREHOUS',,VSAM
// DLBL SYS180,'MGMT.LA.REPORT',30,VSAM,CAT=USER2
// DLBL SYS004,'MGMT.SD.REPORT',30,VSAM,CAT=USER2
// EXEC STATUS2,SIZE=AUTO
/&
```

Naturally, you wouldn't want to retype this job every day, so you decide to turn it into a cataloged procedure. All you have to do is make a few simple changes:

1. Drop the JOB statement.

2. Add a unique symbolic name in columns 73–79 of each statement.

3. Change /& to /+.

The job, now transformed into a procedure, looks like this:

```
// DLBL IJSYSUC,'DEPT.USER.CAT',,VSAM              REP0010
// DLBL SYS220,'INVENTORY.MASTER',,VSAM            REP0020
// DLBL SYS240,'WAREHOUS.ORDERS',,VSAM             REP0030
// DLBL SYS250,'BACK.ORDERS',,VSAM                 REP0040
// DLBL USER2,'USER.CAT.WAREHOUS',,VSAM            REP0050
// DLBL SYS180,'MGMT.LA.REPORT',30,VSAM,CAT=USER2  REP0060
// DLBL SYS004,'MGMT.SD.REPORT',30,VSAM,CAT=USER2  REP0070
// EXEC STATUS2,SIZE=AUTO                          REP0080
/+
```

✓ Check Your Understanding

Change this job to a procedure:

```
// JOB NEWDISK
// ASSGN SYS021,DISK,VOL=999999,SHR
// DLBL DSKFILE,'OUTPUT'
// EXTENT SYS021,999999,1,1,500,200
/&
```

✔ Answer

```
// ASSGN SYS021,DISK,VOL=999999,SHR        DISK001
// DLBL DSKFILE,'OUTPUT'                    DISK002
// EXTENT SYS021,999999,1,1,500,200         DISK003
/+
```

The next step is to catalog the procedure into the Procedure Library. To do that you could use this cataloging job:

```
// JOB FREEDOM
// EXEC MAINT
 CATALP REPORTS
// DLBL IJSYSUC,'DEPT.USER.CAT',,VSAM               REP0010
// DLBL SYS220,'INVENTORY.MASTER',,VSAM             REP0020
// DLBL SYS240,'WAREHOUS.ORDERS',,VSAM              REP0030
// DLBL SYS250,'BACK.ORDERS',,VSAM                  REP0040
// DLBL USER2,'USER.CAT.WAREHOUS',,VSAM             REP0050
// DLBL SYS180,'MGMT.LA.REPORT',30,VSAM,CAT=USER2   REP0060
// DLBL SYS004,'MGMT.SD.REPORT',30,VSAM,CAT=USER2   REP0070
// EXEC STATUS2,SIZE=AUTO                           REP0080
/+
/*
/&
```

Let's go over this job line by line.

The JOB statement starts the job, just as always.

The EXEC statement invokes a program called MAINT, one of VSE's library management programs. MAINT adds a new element to a VSE library (see Figure 7.1). In this case, we're adding a procedure to the Procedure Library. Never use SIZE=AUTO when executing MAINT. Things get mixed up if you do.

Figure 7.1 MAINT's Function

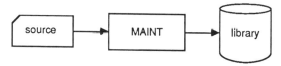

The statements following EXEC, down to /*, are an instream file processed by MAINT. Thus, the JCP does not process all those DLBL statements nor the second EXEC statement; instead, MAINT catalogs them.

The CATALP statement is a *MAINT control statement*, not a

JCL statement. MAINT always expects a unit record file, and the first record must be a control statement telling MAINT what to do. CATALP tells MAINT to *CATALog* the following Procedure. It also names the procedure, in this case REPORTS. Here is the format of the statement:

```
CATALP procedure-name[,VM=v.m][,EOP=yy][,DATA= { NO
                                                 YES }]
```

CATALP is required. It tells the system to catalog a procedure to the Procedure Library. CATALP must start after column 1; column 1 must be blank.

procedure-name is required. It may have up to eight alphameric characters. Procedure-name must not be ALL, and it must not begin with a number or with $$.

The remainder of the operands are keyword, rather than positional; all are optional.

VM = v.m This operand specifies the version number of the procedure. The v (version) may be any decimal number from 0 to 127. The m (modification number) may be any decimal number from 0 to 255. If you omit this operand, the system assumes you're cataloging version 0.0.

EOP = yy This operand allows you to specify an end-of-procedure delimiter other than / + . The only reason to do this is if your procedure contains a statement starting with / + that does *not* mark the end of the procedure (a rare event). You may not use /*, /&, or //; and the delimiter must not include a blank or comma. If you omit the EOP operand, the system assumes you want to use / + .

DATA = YES Use this when the cataloged procedure itself includes instream data. If you omit this operand, or specify DATA = NO, the system assumes there is no instream data. DATA = YES doesn't always work and should be avoided unless you know how it works on your system.

There are some restrictions on the content of the procedures you catalog to the Procedure Library:

1. A procedure may not contain /&.

2. A procedure cannot reassign SYSRDR. If it did, the system couldn't find its way back to the procedure again.

3. For the same reason, a procedure may not contain an EXEC statement that invokes another cataloged procedure.

4. If the procedure contains instream data, it must not reassign SYSIPT. Once again, same reason. The system would get lost.

Sometimes you want to create a set of procedures that all do the same thing, but each is appropriate to a specific partition. You might have six procedures, one appropriate to F1, one to F2, and so forth. The procedure names are the key to making this work. You name the procedures $xyyyyyy, where x indicates the partition: 0 for background and 1–B for foreground. yyyyyy is the name of the procedure, the same name for all the procedures in the set. So if the procedures all edit time cards, you might use the name $0EDTIME for the version designed for the background partition, $1EDTIME for the F1 version, $2EDTIME for the F2 version, and so forth. Now here's the payoff: to execute the appropriate version no matter which partition you're in, EXEC PROC = $$EDTIME. VSE replaces the second $ with the appropriate code for the current partition. Thus, you can submit a job that will execute the appropriate procedure no matter which partition your job ends up in.

✓ Check Your Understanding

1. Catalog the following job, which is version 4.1.

```
// JOB STATEMENTS
// DLBL SYS180,'INFILE',,VSAM
// EXEC MONTHEND,SIZE=AUTO
/&
```

2. What's wrong with these jobs?

```
a. // JOB CATPROC
   // EXEC MAINT
   // ASSGN SYS006,TAPE,VOL=111111          NEWEMP01
   // ASSGN SYS008,DISK                     NEWEMP02
   // TLBL INTAPE,'NEW.EMPL.CHICAGO'        NEWEMP03
   // DLBL OUTDISK,'EMPLOY.MASTER',,VSAM    NEWEMP04
   // EXEC ADDEMPS,SIZE=AUTO                NEWEMP05
   /+
   /*
   /&
```

```
b. // JOB CATPROC
   // EXEC MAINT
      CATALP ADDCHI,VM=1.1,DATA=YES
   // ASSGN SYS006,TAPE,VOL=111111          NEWEMP01
   // ASSGN SYS008,DISK                     NEWEMP02
   // TLBL INTAPE,'NEW.EMPL.CHICAGO'        NEWEMP03
   // DLBL OUTDISK,'EMPLOY.MASTER',,VSAM    NEWEMP04
   // EXEC ADDEMPS,SIZE=AUTO                NEWEMP05
   /+
   /*
   /&
```

```
c. // JOB CATPROC
   // EXEC MAINT
      CATALP ADDCHI,VM=1.1,EOP=..
   // ASSGN SYS006,TAPE,VOL=111111          NEWEMP01
   // ASSGN SYS008,DISK                     NEWEMP02
   // TLBL INTAPE,'NEW.EMPL.CHICAGO'        NEWEMP03
   // DLBL OUTDISK,'EMPLOY.MASTER',,VSAM    NEWEMP04
   // EXEC ADDEMPS,SIZE=AUTO                NEWEMP05
   **
   /*
   /&
```

```
d. // JOB CATPROC
   // EXEC MAINT
      CATALP LOOKOUT
   // ASSGN SYS006,TAPE,VOL=111111          NEWEMP01
   // ASSGN SYS008,DISK                     NEWEMP02
   // ASSGN SYSRDR,DISKETTE,VOL=010123      NEWEMP03
   // EXEC WHERSIT                          NEWEMP04
   /+
   /*
   /&
```

✔ Answers

```
1. // JOB CATALOG
   // EXEC MAINT
      CATALP STMTS,VM=4.1
   // DLBL SYS180,'INFILE',,VSAM          STMT001
   // EXEC MONTHEND,SIZE=AUTO             STMT002
   /+
   /*
   /&
```

2. a. The CATALP statement is missing.
   b. DATA=YES is specified but the procedure contains no in-stream data.
   c. The end-of-procedure delimiter defined in the CATALP statement (..) doesn't match the last line of the instream file (**).
   d. Line NEWEMP03 reassigns SYSRDR. That's a no-no.

Running a Cataloged Procedure

You can try out your REPORTS procedure like this:

```
// JOB TRYIT
// EXEC PROC=REPORTS
/*
```

That's it! Instead of keying that long, dreary job, all you need do is submit this little three-line job, and it is done.

Figure 7.2, on the next page, illustrates how VSE executed this job.

You remember that JCL statements enter the system through SYSRDR. Data statements enter the system through SYSIPT. In the little job above, the JOB statement enters the system through SYSRDR, which is probably assigned to the standard unit record device. Then the EXEC PROC = REPORTS statement enters through SYSRDR. The PROC = operand tells the operating system to reassign SYSRDR to the Procedure Library, to the procedure named REPORTS. The JCP then reads and prcesses the statements in REPORTS, since they are now on SYSRDR.

Figure 7.2 Processing a Cataloged Procedure

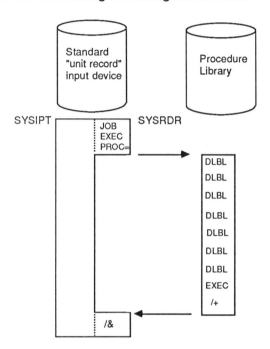

When the procedure statement EXEC STATUS2,SIZE = AUTO is read, the program STATUS2 is loaded and given control. When STATUS2 finishes executing, the JCP reads the next statement in the procedure and finds the / + end-of-procedure delimiter. This causes VSE to *reset* the SYSRDR assignment to whatever it was before. Thus, the next statement the JCP reads is from our little three-line job, which ends the job.

✓ Check Your Understanding

Write a job to invoke the procedure named STMTS that you just cataloged.

✔ Answer

```
// JOB STATEJOB
// EXEC PROC=STMTS
/&
```

Procedures Involving Instream Data

Most procedures involving unit record data do not catalog the unit record data (DATA = NO). They expect you to supply the data when the job is executed by including the appropriate file(s) right after the EXEC PROC= statement. For example:

```
// JOB FORMAT
// EXEC PROC=FORM3
   instream data for FORM3
/*
/&
```

How do you know where to place the instream data? Figure 7.3 illustrates the order in which statements are read. This will help you understand where to place your instream files.

Figure 7.3 Instream Data with a Cataloged Procedure

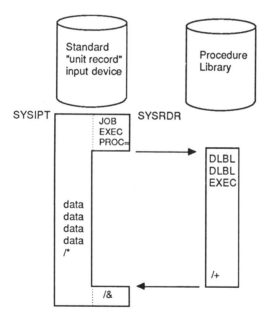

The JCP reads JCL statements from SYSRDR, which usually shares a physical unit with SYSIPT. When EXEC PROC= is encountered, the JCP begins reading JCL statements from the indicated cataloged procedure. However, when a program is executed, it reads from SYSIPT. So, VSE automatically looks to the standard system input device for the unit record data set, which is just where we've placed it.

If the job involves multiple instream files, just line them all up in the order of execution. For example, suppose the PREPLOSS cataloged procedure executes three programs: SORTER, EDITOR, and UPDATER, in that order. Each program requires a unit record input file. Here's how you'd execute the procedure:

```
// JOB DOPREP
// EXEC PROC=PREPLOSS
   instream data for SORTER
/*
   instream data for EDITOR
/*
   instream data for UPDATER
/*
/&
```

If DATA = YES was specified when the job was cataloged, then *all* instream data must be included in the procedure. You can't provide any instream files with the invoking JCL.

✓ Check Your Understanding

1. Write a job to execute the RLOCKS procedure, which requires two unit record input files.

2. Suppose you're cataloging a job requiring only one unit record input file that never changes. Would you use DATA = NO or DATA = YES?

3. Suppose you're cataloging a job requiring two unit record input files. One never changes, but the other will be different each time the job is run. Would you use DATA = NO or DATA = YES?

✔ Answers

1. ```
   //  JOB LOCKUP
   //  EXEC PROC=RLOCKS
       input file #1
   /*
       input file #2
   /*
   /&
   ```

2. DATA=YES

3. DATA=NO

Overriding the Procedure

Now suppose you want to run your REPORTS procedure, but this time (only) you want to make a few changes. The system catalog is to be used in place of DEPT.USER.CAT, and the output file named MGMT.LA.REPORT should be retained 90 days instead of 30.

You're about to discover the purpose of the symbolic names in columns 73 to 79 of each statement. By referring to those symbolic names, you can change any statement you wish. Changing a statement in a cataloged procedure is called *overriding* the statement. The override is temporary; it lasts only until the job is finished. To make the change permanent, you can recatalog the procedure.

You cannot override a statement unless it has a symbolic name in columns 73 to 79. Those symbolic names are not required when you catalog a procedure, but they make the statements overridable, which is desirable. However, if you want to prevent a statement from being overridden, don't give it a symbolic name and no one will be able to override it.

When you override a procedure, you can add, delete, or replace statements. To override a procedure, you add an extra operand (OV) to the EXEC PROC= statement, and then you follow your override statements with an OVEND statement.
   ```

Here's how you would override the REPORTS procedure.

```
// JOB THISTIME
// EXEC PROC=REPORTS,OV
                                                        REP0010D
// DLBL SYS180,'MGMT.LA.REPORT',90,VSAM,CAT=USER2        REP0060R
// OVEND
/&
```

This deletes statement REP0010, which defines a job catalog. It also changes the 30-day retention period to 90 days in REP0060. The symbolic name at the right tells the system which statement to override. A "D" in column 80 says to delete that statement, and an "R" in column 80 says to replace that statement.

If you want to add a statement, you write the statement to be added and include the symbolic name of the cataloged statement before or after the position where you want your new statement to be. If you want your new statement to go before the cataloged statement, put "B" in column 80. If you want your new statement to go after the cataloged statement, put "A" in column 80. Any other letter in column 80 (except "D", which is reserved for deletions) means you want to replace the statement with that symbolic name. We use "R" because it makes sense, but any character other than "A", "B", and "D" will do.

Figure 7.4 depicts VSE processing of a procedure executed with the OV operand.

It starts by reading the first cataloged statement and the first override statement. If the override statement doesn't override the cataloged statement, indicated by matching codes in columns 73 through 79, the first cataloged statement is processed and then the next cataloged statement is read. When the override statement overrides the cataloged statement, the override statement is processed. Then new statements are read from both sources. When the OVEND statement is found, VSE no longer looks for overrides but continues processing the cataloged statements.

Your override statements must appear in the same order as the cataloged statements they refer to. If they get out of order, the statement-matching process will be thrown off and your overrides won't be processed properly. You'll see an example of an incorrect job later in the chapter.

If the job has been cataloged with DATA = YES, you can override the cataloged JCL statements but not the cataloged data records.

Figure 7.4 Processing with Overrides

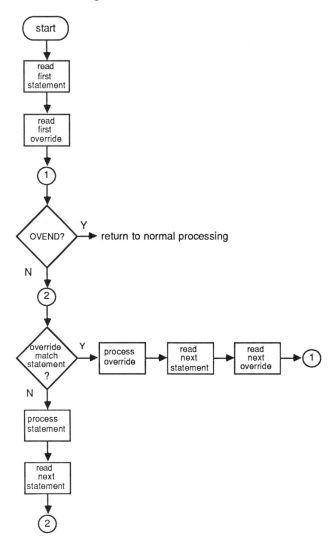

Check Your Understanding

1. Here's a cataloged procedure named LOGGER:

```
// ASSGN SYS005,280,VOL=123000,SHR                      LOG0010
// ASSGN SYS006,281,VOL=124000,SHR                      LOG0020
// DLBL DISKIN,'JOBLOG'                                 LOG0030
// DLBL DISKOUT,'LOGLIST',10                            LOG0040
// EXTENT SYS006,124000,,,400,400                       LOG0050
// EXEC LOGOUT                                          LOG0060
/+
```

Execute this procedure with the following changes:
   a. Eliminate the ASSGN statement for SYS005.
   b. Change the EXTENT statement for SYS006 to use 200 tracks starting at track 780.
   c. Add a second EXTENT statement using 300 tracks starting at track 1000.

2. What's wrong with this job?

```
// JOB LOGJOB
// EXEC PROC=LOGGER,OV
                                                        LOG0050D
                                                        LOG0040D
// OVEND
/&
```

✔ **Answers**

1.
```
// JOB LOGJOB
// EXEC PROC=LOGGER,OV
                                                        LOG0010D
// EXTENT SYS006,124000,,,780,200                       LOG0050R
// EXTENT ,,,,1000,300                                  LOG0050A
// OVEND
/&
```

Your first EXTENT statement could have any character except A, B, or D in column 80. Your second EXTENT statement could have LOG0060B in columns 73–80.

2. The override statements are out of order and the second one will never be processed.

Combining Overrides with Instream Data

Suppose you're invoking a cataloged procedure that needs an instream data file, and you want to override some of the cataloged statements. Both the instream data file and the override statements must follow the EXEC PROC= statement on SYSIPT, but which comes first? Here's where you must keep your wits about you, because you have to put the statements in the order VSE will look for them.

Here's a sample cataloged procedure (INVJOB):

```
// DLBL INVENTY,'WH3.INVENTY',,VSAM                    INV0010
// DLBL PARTS,'WH3.PARTS',,VSAM                        INV0020
// DLBL ORDERS,'WH3.ORDERS',,VSAM                      INV0030
// DLBL OVERAGE,'WH3.OVERAGE',,VSAM                    INV0040
// EXEC CHECKINV,SIZE=AUTO                             INV0050
// DLBL ORDIN,'WH3.ORDERS',,VSAM                       INV0060
// EXEC INVOICE, SIZE=AUTO                             INV0070
/+
```

Suppose both CHECKINV and INVOICE require unit record input. To invoke the procedure with no overrides, you'd enter this job:

```
// JOB JULYINV
// EXEC PROC=INVJOB
   instream data for CHECKINV
/*
   instream data for INVOICE
/*
/&
```

Now suppose you want to run the job using a file named 'WH3.BACKORDS' in place of 'WH3.ORDERS'. Lines INV0030 and INV0060 must be overridden. The two instream files must be positioned so they can be accessed after lines INV0050 and INV0070 are processed. Since the affected lines will be processed in this order: INV0030 (override), INV0050 (instream data), INV0060 (override), and INV0070 (instream data), the correct job is:

```
// JOB JULYINV
// EXEC PROC=INVJOB,OV
// DLBL ORDERS,'WH3.BACKORDS',,VSAM                    INV0030R
   instream data for CHECKINV
/*
// DLBL ORDIN,'WH3.BACKORDS',,VSAM                     INV0060R
// OVEND
   instream data for INVOICE
/*
/&
```

If these statements were in any other order, VSE would not read them at the correct time, and the job would fail. For example, suppose you submitted this job instead:

```
// JOB JULYINV
// EXEC PROC=INVJOB,OV
// DLBL ORDER,'WH3.BACKORDS',,VSAM          INV0030R
// DLBL ORDIN,'WH3.BACKORDS',,VSAM          INV0060R
// OVEND
   instream data for CHECKINV
/*
   instream data for INVOICE
/*
/&
```

Here's what would happen. VSE would process lines INV0010 and INV0020 properly. It would find the override for line INV0030 and process that properly. Then it would process lines INV0040 and INV0050 properly. Line INV0050 invokes the CHECKINV program, which assumes control. CHECKINV reads a record from the unit record file on SYSIPT. What does it get? The next record from SYSRDR:

```
// DLBL ORDIN,'WH3.BACKORDS',,VSAM          INV0060R
```

CHECKINV tries to process this as an input data record. Hopefully it causes CHECKINV to bomb and the job fails immediately. But let's look at the worst case: CHECKINV accepts and processes the record, putting bad data in the output files (ORDERS and OVERAGE). The next "record" it processes is:

```
   // OVEND
```

More bad output data. Now CHECKINV gets to the real instream data and terminates normally when it reaches the /* statement. VSE regains control and reads line INV0060. It finds no override for this statement; remember that the override was processed as an input data record by CHECKINV. Therefore, the INVOICE program tries to use 'WH3.ORDERS' as ORDIN. The best result: no 'WH3.ORDERS' exists and INVOICE abends. The worst result: an old version of 'WH3.ORDERS' is used, complicating the mess even more; the job doesn't fail, so no one notices; the user ignores the one symptom of the problem, a warning message saying no OVEND statement was found.

Why did we walk you through this? To help you understand the order in which VSE processes the statements and the problems that can happen when they're in the wrong order. And incidentally to point out how important warning messages are, even if they seem minor and stupid. ("What do you mean, no OVEND statement was found? It's right there on line five. VSE is crazy.")

VSE has one rule that occasionally changes the order of overrides and instream data. When OV appears on an EXEC statement, the next statement must be an override statement, even if that changes the normal sequence of the statements. Reexamine the diagram in Figure 7.4 and you'll see why. For example, suppose you want to execute INVJOB with two changes for the second step only. ORDIN should be assigned to 'TEST.ORDERS' and SYS020 should be assigned to unit 181. Here's the correct job:

```
// JOB  JULYINV
// EXEC PROC=INVJOB,OV
// ASSGN SYS020,181                          INV0060B
   instream data for CHECKINV
/*
// DLBL ORDIN,'TEST.ORDERS',,VSAM            INV0060R
// OVEND
   instream data for INVOICE
/*
/&
```

The ASSGN statement precedes the first instream file for only one reason: because the first record after the EXEC statement must be an override.

✓ Check Your Understanding

1. Write a job to execute INVJOB but retain the two output files (ORDERS and OVERAGE) 90 days.

2. Write a job to execute INVJOB but delete the second step.

✔ Answers

```
1. // JOB TESTINV
   // EXEC PROC=INVJOB,OV
   // DLBL ORDERS,'WH3.ORDERS',90,VSAM                    INV0030R
   // DLBL OVERAGE,'WH3.OVERAGE',90,VSAM                  INV0040R
   // OVEND
      instream data for CHECKINV
   /*
      instream data for INVOICE
   /*
   /&


2. // JOB TESTINV
   // EXEC PROC=INVJOB,OV
                                                          INV0060D
      instream data for CHECKINV
   /*
                                                          INV0070D
   // OVEND
   /&
```

Finding Out What's in the Library

VSE includes some library utility programs that tell you what's in a library. DSERV displays the directory of one or more libraries. PSERV displays the contents of one or more procedures in the Procedure Library, CSERV accesses the Core Image Library, ESERV and SSERV access the Source Statement Library, and RSERV accesses the Relocatable Library.

Using DSERV

To list the names of the elements in a library, execute the DSERV utility with EXEC DSERV (see Figure 7.5). DSERV requires at least one control statement telling which library(ies) to display and whether or not to sort the names. Here's the format of the statement:

```
DSPLY[S]  directory[,directory ... ]
```

Figure 7.5 Function of DSERV

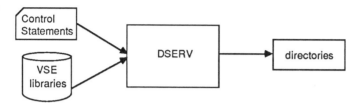

If you code DSPLY, the names are not sorted; with DSPLYS, they are. Column one of the control statement must be blank. The directories you can display are:

CD   Core Image Library directory

RD   Relocatable Library directory

PD   Procedure Library directory

SD   Source Statement Library directory

SDL   System Directory List

ALL   All of the above

(Some more options exist for the Core Image Library. You might want to look them up in your reference manual later.)

Suppose you want to list the names of the procedures in the Procedure Library in alphabetical order. Here's the job:

```
// JOB PROCLIST
// EXEC DSERV
   DSPLYS PD
/*
/&
```

Don't forget the control statements count as instream data and must be followed by /*.

Using PSERV

To list one or more cataloged procedures (the contents, not just the names), execute the PSERV utility with EXEC PSERV (see

Figure 7.6). Its control statement looks like this:

$$\begin{Bmatrix} DSPLY \\ PUNCH \\ DSPCH \end{Bmatrix}, \begin{Bmatrix} name[,name \ ...] \\ ALL \end{Bmatrix}$$

Figure 7.6 Function of PSERV

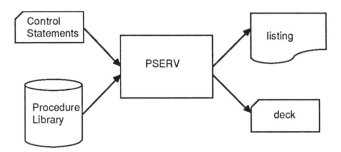

DSPLY lists the procedure, PUNCH punches it, and DSPCH does both. ALL produces the entire library, which could be a lengthy job but you may need to do it if you have no other way of finding out what procedures are available to you. Here's a job that lists three procedures:

```
// JOB LISTPROC
// EXEC PSERV
   DSPLY LOSTJOB,FOUNDJOB,DELEJOB
/*
/&
```

✅ Check Your Understanding

1. Write a job to list all the alphabetized directories of all the system libraries.

2. Write a job to list the contents of the procedure named MARKIT.

3. Write a job to list the contents of all procedures in the system Procedure Library.

✔ **Answers**

1.
```
// JOB LIBDIRS
// EXEC DSERV
   DSPLYS ALL
/*
/&
```

2.
```
// JOB LISTMARK
// EXEC PSERV
   DSPLY MARKIT
/*
/&
```

3.
```
// JOB LISTPL
// EXEC PSERV
   DSPLY ALL
/*
/&
```

The other library service programs, such as CSERV and RSERV, are used in a fashion similar to RSERV. Check your JCL reference manual for details if you want to use them.

Using Private Procedure Libraries

You learned in Chapter 6 how to access private libraries. By way of review, here's a job that accesses a cataloged procedure in the private library named ACCTPL:

```
// JOB RUNACCT
// LIBDEF PL,SEARCH=(ACCTPL)
// EXEC PROC=NEWACCT
/&
```

How do you get the procedure into the private library? Use LIBDEF in the MAINT job. But instead of SEARCH=, use TO=. Here's a sample job that catalogs NEWACCT to the ACCTPL library.

```
// JOB CATACCT
// LIBDEF PL,TO=ACCTPL
// EXEC MAINT
   CATALP NEWACCT
   instream data (NEWACCT procedure)
/*
/&
```

To find out what's in a private library, use the LIBDEF FROM= option with xSERV. Here's an example:

```
// JOB FINDOUT
// LIBDEF PL,FROM=ACCTPL
// EXEC DSERV
   DSPLYS PD
/*
/&
```

This job lists the names of all the procedures in the ACCTPL library.

Here's the format of LIBDEF showing the TO= and FROM= options:

$$// \text{ LIBDEF } \begin{Bmatrix} \text{CL} \\ \text{RL} \\ \text{SL} \\ \text{PL} \end{Bmatrix} , \begin{Bmatrix} \text{SEARCH=(name[,...])} \\ \text{FROM=name} \\ \text{TO=name} \end{Bmatrix} \begin{bmatrix} \text{,TEMP} \\ \text{,PERM} \end{bmatrix}$$

If any permanent LIBDEF SEARCH= chains are assigned to your partition, you'll have to specify a LIBDEF TO= or FROM= statement for your MAINT and xSERV jobs, or the jobs will fail.

✓ Check Your Understanding

1. Write a job to catalog a procedure named LOSTACCT to the private library named SALESPL.

2. Now write a job to execute that procedure. (No instream data needed.)

3. Write a job to list the contents of that procedure.

✔ Answers

1. ```
   // JOB CATALJOB
   // LIBDEF PL,TO=SALESPL
   // EXEC MAINT
      CATALP LOSTACCT
      instream data
   /*
   /&
   ```

2. ```
   // JOB LOSTJOB
   // LIBDEF PL,SEARCH=(SALESPL)
   // EXEC PROC=LOSTACCT
   /&
   ```

3. ```
   // JOB LISTPROC
   // LIBDEF PL,FROM=SALESPL
   // EXEC PSERV
      DSPLY LOSTACCT
   /*
   /&
   ```
   ```

Chapter Summary

In this chapter, you've learned how to create, catalog, and use cataloged procedures. Convert a job into a cataloged procedure by: (1) removing the JOB statement; (2) adding a symbolic name to columns 73–79 of each overridable statement; and (3) changing /& to / + . Catalog the job by executing MAINT with a CATALP control statement. Execute the job by EXEC PROC = . Put any necessary instream data files after the EXEC statement unless the procedure has been cataloged with DATA = YES, in which case all instream files must be cataloged with the procedure.

Override cataloged statements by adding OV to the EXEC statement and placing override statements after the EXEC statement. Use the symbolic name in columns 73–79 to identify the statement to be overridden. Column 80 should contain A to add the override statement after the overridden statement, B to add the override statement before the overridden statement, D to delete the overridden statement, and any other code to replace the overridden statement. If your invoking job contains both override statements and instream files, be sure to put them in the order VSE processes the cataloged statements, but one override statement must immediately follow the EXEC statement.

To find out what's in the Procedure Library, execute DSERV and PSERV. DSERV displays any library directory; PSERV displays procedures. Each program requires at least one control statement indicating what you want displayed. RSERV, CSERV, SSERV, and ESERV provide similar functions for the other libraries.

You can access private libraries by preceding the EXEC statement with a LIBDEF statement. Use the SEARCH = operand to execute a procedure from a private library (with EXEC PROC =). Use TO = to catalog a procedure to a private library (with MAINT). Use FROM = to find out what's in a private library (with xSERV).

✓ Chapter Exercise

You will use the following job throughout this exercise:

```
// JOB CONVERT
// ASSGN SYS006,TAPE,VOL=111111
// ASSGN SYS007,TAPE,VOL=111222
// TLBL TAPEIN,'REJECTS'
// TLBL TAPEOUT,'GOODRECS'
// EXEC EDITRECS
// ASSGN SYS008,DISK
// ASSGN SYS009,DISK
// DLBL DISKIN,'MASTER.EMPLOYEE.DATA',,VSAM
// DLBL DISKOUT,'SELECTED.EMPLOYEE.DATA',,VSAM
// TLBL CHANGES,'GOODRECS'
// EXEC FIXRECS,SIEE=AUTO
/&
```

1. Convert the job to a procedure.

2. Write the job to catalog this procedure.

3. Rewrite your preceding job to catalog the procedure to a private library named EMPPL.

   From now on, assume that the procedure is cataloged in EMPPL.

4. Write a job to execute the procedure. Both steps require in-stream files.

5. Execute the procedure again. This time reassign the tape files to disk, controlled by VSAM. (You can use the same names.)

6. Execute the procedure again. This time, change the name of DISKIN to 'MASTER.TEMPORY.DATA'.

7. Write a job to list the alphabetized directory of EMPPL.

8. Write a job to list your procedure.

✔ Answers to Chapter Exercise

```
1. // ASSGN SYS006,TAPE,VOL=111111                          CON0010
   // ASSGN SYS007,TAPE,VOL=111222                          CON0020
   // TLBL TAPEIN,'REJECTS'                                 CON0030
   // TLBL TAPEOUT,'GOODRECS'                               CON0040
   // EXEC EDITRECS                                         CON0050
   // ASSGN SYS008,DISK                                     CON0060
   // ASSGN SYS009,DISK                                     CON0070
   // DLBL DISKIN,'MASTER.EMPLOYEE.DATA',,VSAM              CON0080
   // DLBL DISKOUT,'SELECTED.EMPLOYEE.DATA',,VSAM           CON0090
   // TLBL CHANGES,'GOODRECS'                               CON0100
   // EXEC FIXRECS,SIZE=AUTO                                CON0110
   /+

2. // JOB CATPROC
   // EXEC MAINT
      CATALP CONVERT
      instream data
   /*
   /&

3. // JOB CATPROC
   // LIBDEF PL,TO=EMPPL
   // EXEC MAINT
      CATALP CONVERT
      instream data
   /*
   /&

4. // JOB CONJOB
   // LIBDEF PL,SEARCH=(EMPPL)
   // EXEC PROC=CONVERT
      (instream file for EDITRECS)
   /*
      (instream file for FIXRECS)
   /*
   /&

5. // JOB CONJOB
   // LIBDEF PL,SEARCH=(EMPPL)
   // EXEC PROC=CONVERT,OV
   // ASSGN SYS006,DISK                                     CON0010R
   // ASSGN SYS007,DISK                                     CON0020R
   // DLBL TAPEIN,'REJECTS',,VSAM                           CON0030R
   // DLBL TAPEOUT,'GOODRECS',,VSAM                         CON0040R
      (instream file for EDITRECS)
   /*
   // DLBL CHANGES,'GOODRECS',,VSAM                         CON0100R
   // OVEND
      (instream file for FIXRECS)
   /*
   /&
```

```
6. // JOB CONJOB
   // LIBDEF PL,SEARCH=(EMPPL)
   // EXEC PROC=CONVERT,OV
   // DLBL DISKIN,'MASTER.TEMPORY.DATA',,VSAM          CON0080R
      (instream file for EDITRECS)
   /*
      (instream file for FIXRECS)
   /*
   /&

7. // JOB WHATPL
   // LIBDEF PL,FROM=EMPPL
   // EXEC DSERV
      DSPLYS PD
   /*
   /&

8. // JOB LISTPROC
   // LIBDEF PL,FROM=EMPPL
   // EXEC PSERV
      DSPLY CONVERT
   /*
   /&
```

Compiling, Assembling, and Linking

As a programmer, the jobs you run most often involve compiling or assembling, linking, and testing. You'll run these jobs in various combinations. When you first write a program, you'll probably compile it without linking or testing, as a syntax check. Once you've got a clean compile, you'll probably run a compile-link-go job to test the program. You continue to run compile-link-go jobs until the program is completely debugged. Then you'll run a compile-link job that catalogs the phase into the Core Image Library.

This chapter shows you how to create all these types of jobs. You'll learn how to execute compilers and the linkage editor. In addition, you'll learn how to control various options these programs offer. When you have completed this chapter, you'll be able to:

✔   Write an OPTION statement to control compilation and linkage editing

✔   Write a PHASE statement to name a phase

✔   Write an ACTION statement to control the linkage editor

✔   Write a compile only (syntax check) job

✔   Write a compile-link-go job

✔   Write a compile-link-catalog job

✔   Use private libraries when compiling, linking, and cataloging

✔   Use cataloged procedures for these jobs

Using a Compiler

No matter which compiler or assembler you want to use, the process is the same as far as your JCL is concerned. We'll use the COBOL compiler in our examples, but don't be concerned if you want to use Fortran, PL/I, or the system assembler; only the name on the EXEC statement is different.

The input to the compiler is a source program in the form of a unit record file (see Figure 8.1). We'll show the instream file in our jobs, but don't forget that if you have ICCF you can IN-CLUDE the file in your job, which is a lot more convenient.

Figure 8.1 Compiler/Assembler I/O

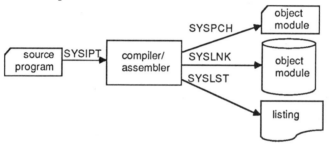

The compiler has two possible outputs: an object module (if no severe errors are found) and a listing on SYSLST, which contains many different features you can control through your JCL. The object module, if issued, can be "punched" as a "deck of cards" on SYSPCH (most likely stored in card image format on a disk file), and it can be written to SYSLNK, a system logical unit used solely as input to the linkage editor. You'll "punch" a "deck" if you want to catalog the object module in the Relocatable Library. You'll write the output to SYSLNK if you want to link edit it. For syntax checks, you'll do neither, since no object module is needed.

Don't worry about ASSGN and DLBL statements for compilers. Your installation has stored permanent ones for all the necessary files. The only time you would need to define one is if you want to override your installation's defaults.

Never specify SIZE=AUTO when using any compiler, the assembler, or the linkage editor. It goofs them up.

Syntax Checking

To check the syntax of a new source program, compile it without producing an object program (see Figure 8.2). Here's a sample job:

Figure 8.2 Syntax Checking

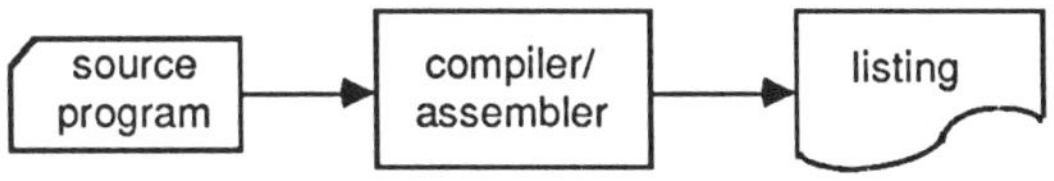

```
// JOB SYNTAX
// OPTION NOLINK,NODECK
// EXEC FCOBOL
   source program
/*
/&
```

As you probably guessed, it's the OPTION statement that does the trick. In this case, we requested NOLINK (don't put the output on SYSLNK) and NODECK (don't punch a deck). Hence no object module is issued. The only output is the listing.

Controlling the Listing

Other OPTION parameters control the contents of the listing. Here are some you can choose from:

LIST/NOLIST   Controls whether or not the listing is produced. If you choose LIST, you get at least a source program listing. What else you get depends on the other parameters you use. When you choose NOLIST, the other parameters that affect the listing don't work.

ERRS/NOERRS   Controls whether error messages are included in the compiler listing (they're automatically included in assembler listings).

The following parameters are useful mostly in debugging.

You'll probably need a system programmer to help you interpret the listings produced.

LISTX/NOLISTX   Object module listing

RLD/NORLD   Relocation directory (assembler only)

XREF/SXREF/ NOXREF   Cross-reference listing

SYM/NOSYM   Symbol table

A standard syntax check job looks something like this:

```
// JOB SYNTAX
// OPTION NODECK,NOLINK,LIST,ERRS,NOLISTX,NORLD,NOSYM,NOXREF
// EXEC FCOBOL
   source program
/*
/&
```

Your installation has selected default values for each option. Find out what they are. You don't need to specify options unless you want to override the defaults. For example, suppose your system defaults are NODECK, LINK, LIST, ERRS, NOLISTX, NORLD, NOSYM, and XREF. You could recode the preceding OPTION statement like this:

```
// OPTION NOLINK,NOXREF
```

The options you select are temporary. They last only until another OPTION statement is encountered or the job ends.

Be sure to put the OPTION statement before the EXEC statement for the compiler or assembler.

✓ Check Your Understanding

1. Assume your installation has these default options: NODECK, NOLINK, LIST, NOERRS, NOLISTX, NORLD, NOSYM, NOXREF. Write a job to do a standard syntax check.

2. What's wrong with these jobs?

```
a. // JOB COBCOMP
   // OPTION NOLINK,NODECK,NOLIST
   // EXEC FCOBOL
      source program
   /*
   /&
```

```
b. // JOB COBCOMP
   // OPTION NOLIST,ERRS,LISTX,XREF,SYM
   // EXEC FCOBOL
      source program
   /*
   /&
```

```
c. // JOB COBCOMP
   // OPTION LIST
   // EXEC FCOBOL
   /&
```

✔ **Answers**

```
1. // JOB SYNTAX
   // OPTION ERRS
   // EXEC FCOBOL
      source program
   /*
   /&
```

(You can include default options if you wish.)

2. a. The OPTION statement requests no output at all from the compiler.
   b. ERRS, LISTX, XREF, and SYM won't be printed when NOLIST is chosen.
   c. No source program is provided; FCOBOL has nothing to compile.

Compile-Link-Go

Now let's produce an object module, pass it to the linkage editor, produce a temporary phase, and execute the phase (see Figure 8.3 on the following page).

Figure 8.3 Compile-Link-Go Job

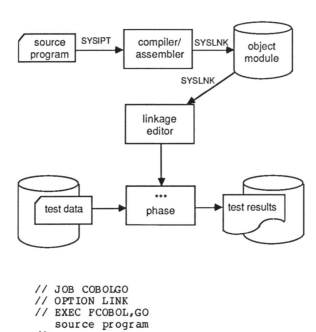

```
// JOB COBOLGO
// OPTION LINK
// EXEC FCOBOL,GO
   source program
/*
   test input
/*
/&
```

The LINK option makes SYSLNK available to the job. The compiler places the object module on SYSLNK; the linkage editor finds it there. (This is the sole function of SYSLNK.) OPTION LINK is required when you want to use the linkage editor. The object module is automatically deleted from SYSLNK at the end of the job.

Notice the GO operand on the EXEC statement. This tells VSE to link edit and then execute the program. It's shorthand for EXEC LNKEDT followed by EXEC with *** implied. In fact, this is actually a three-step job, although only one EXEC statement shows. The phase is automatically deleted from the Core Image Library at the end of the job.

The third step, when the phase is executed, probably requires test data. In our example, we've shown a unit record input file. But more files may be involved, and the job must include whatever ASSGN, TLBL, DLBL, and EXTENT statements necessary to identify the proper files for the program.

Check Your Understanding

1. Write a job to compile and test a program that requires only one unit record input file.

2. What's wrong with these jobs?

   a.
```
// JOB COBOLGO
// OPTION NODECK,NOLINK
// EXEC FCOBOL,GO
   source program
/*
   input file
/*
/&
```

   b.
```
// JOB COBOLGO
// OPTION LINK
// EXEC FCOBOL
   source program
/*
/&
```

✔ **Answers**

1.
```
// JOB COBOLGO
// OPTION LINK
// EXEC FCOBOL,GO
   source program
/*
   unit record input
/*
/&
```

2. a. The GO operand requests linkage editing, so the LINK option must be selected.
   b. Option LINK is selected but the linkage editor isn't used. The object module will be placed on SYSLNK, then erased from SYSLNK without ever being used.

Compile, Link, and Catalog

Suppose you've debugged your program, and it's ready to go into production. It's time to put the phase in the Core Image Library (see Figure 8.4). Here's the job:

Figure 8.4 Compile-Link-Catalog Job

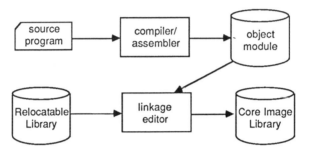

```
// JOB CATPROG
// LIBDEF CL,TO=COMLIB
// OPTION CATAL,NOLIST
   PHASE $DROPS,*
// EXEC FCOBOL
   source program
/*
// EXEC LINKEDT
/&
```

The LIBDEF statement is necessary to name the private library to receive the new phase.

The CATAL option tells the linkage editor to catalog the phase in the Core Image Library. It implies LINK, making SYSLNK available, so you never need to code LINK when CATAL is used. You can code other options (except NOLINK) with CATAL; we've shown NOLIST as an example.

The PHASE statement is a linkage editor control statement. It assigns a name to the program and specifies its memory location. Unlike other control statements you've seen, it's not contained in a unit record input file. You simply include it in the job, and the JCP transfers it to SYSLNK. On SYSLNK, it must *precede* the object module. Thus you must put it before the

EXEC FCOBOL statement that puts the object module on SYSLNK.

Here's the format for the PHASE statement:

```
PHASE phasename,location
```

The first column must be blank.

The phase name can have up to eight characters. Start it with $ if you're cataloging it to the system Core Image Library. Otherwise, don't start it with $. Don't use the names ALL, S, or ROOT, as they have special meanings.

The location dictates where the program will be loaded in memory whenever it's executed. You can specify this by memory address or by partition. If you don't care, use *. This makes the program relocatable; that is, each time it's executed, VSE puts it in the most convenient location. This is the best option and you should use it whenever possible. If you do have to limit a program to a specific partition or a specific memory area, get help from a system programmer.

✓ Check Your Understanding

1. Write a job to compile, link, and catalog a program named $PERT. Make it relocatable.

2. What's wrong with these jobs?

   a.
   ```
   // JOB CATPHASE
   // OPTION CATAL,NOLINK
      PHASE UNDERPAY,*
   // EXEC FCOBOL
      source program
   /*
   // EXEC LNKEDT
   /&
   ```

   b.
   ```
   // JOB CATPHASE
      PHASE UNDERPAY,*
   // EXEC FCOBOL
      source program
   /*
   // OPTION CATAL
   // EXEC LNKEDT
   /&
   ```

```
c. // JOB CATPHASE
   // OPTION CATAL
      PHASE UNDERPAY,*
   // EXEC FCOBOL,GO
      source program
   /*
   /&

d. // JOB CATPHASE
   // OPTION CATAL
   // EXEC FCOBOL
      source program
   /*
      PHASE UNDERPAY,*
   // EXEC LNKEDT
   /&
```

✔ Answers

```
1. // JOB CATPROG
   // OPTION CATAL
      PHASE $PERT,*
   // EXEC FCOBOL
      source program
   /*
   // EXEC LNKEDT
   /&
```

You might have selected additional options.

2. a. CATAL implies LINK, so you can't specify NOLINK with CATAL.

   b. The OPTION CATAL statement needs to precede the EXEC FCOBOL statement or FCOBOL won't put the object module on SYSLNK.

   c. The GO option looks for a phase named *** in the Core Image Library, but this job catalogs a phase named UNDER-PAY.

   d. The PHASE statement must precede EXEC FCOBOL or it won't be copied onto SYSLNK *before* the object module.

Linkage Editor Listings

Your linkage editor can produce a listing (called a map) on SYSLST, controlled by the ACTION statement, another linkage editor control statement. Generally, the listing won't be useful unless you're a system programmer trying to debug a difficult case. If the listing is included by default at your installation, you can suppress it with this statement:

```
ACTION NOMAP
```

It should be *before* the PHASE statement and immediately after the OPTION statement in your job. If you want to produce the map, get some help in writing the correct ACTION statement and interpreting the output.

Using Private Libraries

Figure 8.5 reviews the use of libraries in compilation, link editing, and testing. So far all the jobs you've worked with in this chapter have used the system libraries. Let's review how to use private libraries.

Figure 8.5 Use of Libraries

Step	Input Library	Output Library
Compilation/assembly	Source Statement	None[1]
Link editing	Relocatable	Core Image
Testing	Core Image	None[2]

1. Compilers and assemblers do not catalog modules directly into the Relocatable Library; MAINT must be used for that purpose.
2. Unless MAINT is the phase being run.

Suppose you're compiling, linking, and testing a program that calls object modules in the private Relocatable Library named TESTRL. Here's how you'd access the library:

```
// JOB COBOLGO
// LIBDEF RL,SEARCH=(TESTRL)
// OPTION LINK
// EXEC FCOBOL,GO
   source program
/*
   test file
/*
/&
```

The LIBDEF statement tells VSE to look *first* in TESTRL for object modules. If a desired module is not found there, VSE searches the permanent chain, if one exists, and then the system library.

Suppose you want to catalog a program to the private Core Image Library named TESTCL. Here's the job:

```
// JOB CATPHASE
// LIBDEF CL,TO=TESTCL
// OPTION CATAL
   PHASE SORTSTDS,*
// EXEC FCOBOL
   source program
/*
// EXEC LINKEDT
/&
```

Here the LIBDEF statement tells VSE to catalog the phase to the private Core Image Library named TESTCL.

✓ Check Your Understanding

1. Write a job to compile, link, and catalog a phase using a private Relocatable Library named TRAINRL and a private Core Image Library named TRAINCL. Name the phase EDUDOC and make it relocatable. Suppress the linkage editor map.

2. What's wrong with these jobs?

   a.
   ```
   // JOB CATPHASE
   // OPTION CATAL
      PHASE NEWLIST,*
      ACTION NOMAP
   // EXEC FCOBOL
      source program
   /*
   // EXEC LNKEDT
   /&
   ```

b.
```
// JOB NEWPHASE
// OPTION LINK
   ACTION NOMAP
// LIBDEF CL,TO=NEWCIL
// EXEC FCOBOL,GO
   source program
/*
   test input
/*
/&
```

✔ Answers

1.
```
// JOB CATPHASE
// LIBDEF RL,SEARCH=(TRAINRL)
// LIBDEF CL,TO=TRAINCL
// OPTION CATAL
   ACTION NOMAP
   PHASE EDUDOC,*
// EXEC FCOBOL
   source program
/*
// EXEC LNKEDT
/&
```

2. a. If used, the ACTION statement must precede the PHASE statement.
   b. The LIBDEF statement makes no sense since the only thing that's cataloged to a Core Image Library is a temporary phase named *** that's automatically deleted at the end of the job.

Using Cataloged Procedures

Your installation probably has cataloged procedures for syntax checks and compile-link-go jobs. You can use those procedures to save time.

Suppose your installation has cataloged this procedure under the name COBSYNTX:

```
// OPTION NOLINK,NODECK,LIST,ERRS          SYS0010
// EXEC FCOBOL                             SYS0020
/*
```

Now how do you do a syntax check on a COBOL program? Here's an example:

```
// JOB SYNTAX
// EXEC PROC=COBSYNTX
   source program
/*
/&
```

Here's a sample compile-link-go procedure named CGO:

```
// OPTION LINK, LIST, ERRS, NODECK                    CGO0010
   ACTION NOMAP                                       CGO0020
// EXEC FCOBOL,GO                                     CGO0030
/*
```

To execute it:

```
// JOB TEST
   I/O statements
// EXEC PROC=CGO
   source program
/*
/&
```

To override it:

```
// JOB TESTOV
   I/O statements
// EXEC PROC=CGO,OV
// OPTION LINK, LIST, ERRS, XREF, RLD, NODECK         CGO0010R
// OVEND
   source program
/*
/&
```

You may want to devise cataloged procedures of your own to save work and specify the options and private libraries you use a great deal.

Chapter Summary

This chapter has shown you how to compile (or assemble), link, test, and catalog a program. Generally you control the process with an OPTION statement preceding the EXEC statement that executes the compiler. For compilation only, select options LIST, NODECK, and NOLINK. You might select other options of items to be included in the listing: ERRS, LISTX, RLD, XREF, and SYM.

To compile-link-go, select option LINK and add the GO option to the EXEC statement. You might also want to suppress the linkage editor listing by including ACTION NOMAP before the EXEC statement. You'll probably need to define I/O files for the GO step.

To compile-link-catalog, select option CATAL and include a PHASE statement before you execute the compiler. (If you have both PHASE and ACTION statements in a job, ACTION goes first.) The second step should be EXEC LNKEDT.

To use private libraries, include a LIBDEF statement in the job. Use SEARCH= to access private libraries (Source Statement for the compiler, Relocatable for the linkage editor) and TO= to catalog (OPTION CATAL with linkage editor).

✓ Chapter Exercise

Assume the default options for your installation are: NODECK, LINK, LIST, ERRS, XREF, NORLD, NOSYM, LISTX.

1. Write a job to do a syntax check on a source program. Use the private Source Statement Library named DUOSSL.

2. Write a job to compile-link-go a source program that uses two disk files (SYS006 and SYS007). For testing purposes, redirect the disk files to unit record. Use DUOSSL and DUORL (Relocatable Library).

3. Write a job to compile-link-catalog the same program, using DUOSSL, DUORL, and DUOCIL (Core Image Library). Name the program SCRIPTER and make it relocatable.

✔ Answers to Chapter Exercise

```
1. // JOB SYNTAX
   // LIBDEF SL,SEARCH=(DUOSSL)
   // OPTION NOLINK,NOXREF,NOLISTX
   // EXEC FCOBOL
      source program
   /*
   /&

2. // JOB CLG
   // LIBDEF SL,SEARCH=(DUOSSL)
   // LIBDEF RL,SEARCH=(DUORL)
   // OPTION NOXREF,NOLISTX
      ACTION NOMAP
   // ASSGN SYS006,SYSIPT
   // ASSGN SYS007,SYSLST
   // EXEC FCOBOL,GO
      source program
   /*
      input file (SYS006)
   /*
   /&

3. // JOB CATPHASE
   // LIBDEF SL,SEARCH=(DUOSSL)
   // LIBDEF RL,SEARCH=(DUORL)
   // LIBDEF CL,TO=DUOCIL
   // OPTION CATAL,NOLIST
      ACTION NOMAP
      PHASE SCRIPTER,*
   // EXEC FCOBOL
      source program
   /*
   // EXEC LNKEDT
   /&
```

Additional JCL Statements

You've learned the most common JCL statements, the ones you'll use every day. But you should be familiar with some of the other available statements; they can come in handy in special situations. This chapter overviews these statements: DATE, UPSI, PAUSE, MTC, LIBDROP, LIBLIST, LISTIO, and SETPRT. You'll also see some new parameters for ASSGN and EXEC.

When you have completed this chapter, you'll be able to:

✔ Identify the functions of the DATE, UPSI, PAUSE, MTC, LIBDROP, LIBLIST, LISTIO, and SETPRT statements

✔ Code DATE, UPSI, and PAUSE statements

✔ Code simple applications of MTC, LIBDROP, LIBLIST, LISTIO, and SETPRT statements

✔ Use the UA, IGN, and ALT parameters on the ASSGN statement

✔ Use the REAL parameter of the EXEC statement

The DATE Statement

When the system is IPL'd, the operator enters the current date and time. This sets the system's clock. All system output is time and date stamped; new tape and disk files have creation and expiration dates stored in their labels; any program can access the date and time for whatever purpose. So the system clock is constantly used.

As a programmer, you can temporarily override the current date and replace it with the date of your choice for a job by using the // DATE statement. (There is one exception: DASD output file labels always use the date set by the operator.) Why would you want to do this? Probably to imply that a job was run on a different day, earlier or later than the real date.

The DATE statement has two permissible formats:

```
// DATE mm/dd/yy          example:   // DATE 01/31/84
                   or
// DATE dd/mm/yy          example:   // DATE 31/01/84
```

The first is American standard format; the second is European. Use the appropriate format for your system, depending on how it usually expresses the date.

The DATE statement is temporary and affects only your current job.

✓ Check Your Understanding

1. Write the statement to change the system date to October 31, 1985, using American format.

2. Write the statement again, using European format.

3. What is affected by the above statements?
   a. All partitions until the system is re-IPL'd
   b. This partition only, until the system is re-IPL'd
   c. This partition only, this job only

✔ Answers

1. // DATE 10/31/85

2. // DATE 31/10/85

3. c

Communicating with Programs

VSE gives each partition a small portion of memory called the communication region. It's cleared at the beginning of each job, and then the job can use it for its own purposes. It's used to provide external information to a program. The operator can pass information to a program through the communication region; the system provides information to a program in the communication region (for example, the date and time are stored in the communication region); one program in a job can leave a message in the communication region for a later program in the same job.

Suppose you have a program that sorts and edits input records, creating an input file for the next step. It passes the number of records in the file to the next program in the job, which uses that information to define a table.

Here's how you'd do it in COBOL:

First program
```
MOVE RECORD-TOTAL TO COM-REG.
```

Second program
```
MOVE COM-REG TO TABLE-LIMIT.
```

The keyword COM-REG is automatically defined to refer to an 11-byte field in the communication region that can contain any type of data. No JCL is involved in this program-to-program communication.

You can also pass data from your JCL to a program. The communication region includes a set of eight on-off switches

called the User Program Switch Indicators (UPSI). Any program can test these switches and make decisions according to
their status. The switches can be set by your JCL.

Suppose you're writing an accounting program that includes
quarterly report and annual report modules. How will your
program decide when to execute those modules? One way could
be to have your program check the UPSI byte. If UPSI-0 is on,
do a quarterly report. If UPSI-1 is on, do an annual report.
Here's how you check the UPSI byte in COBOL:

```
SPECIAL-NAMES.
        UPSI-0 ON STATUS IS QUARTERLY-REPORT.
        UPSI-1 ON STATUS IS ANNUAL-REPORT.
  ...
        IF QUARTERLY-REPORT
            PERFORM PREPARE-QUARTERLY-REPORT.
        IF ANNUAL-REPORT
            PERFORM PREPARE-ANNUAL-REPORT.
```

The UPSI Statement

At the beginning of every job, VSE sets all eight bits of the UPSI
byte to zeros. When the JCP reads your UPSI statement, it sets
the bits in the UPSI byte to correspond with your UPSI statement. You set each bit in your UPSI statement by using 0, 1, or
X like this:

Example 1: // UPSI 11000110

Example 2: // UPSI XX11100X (X means that those bits are unchanged
from the previous UPSI statement.)

Example 3: // UPSI 11111 (The system assumes the three unspeci-
fied bits to the right are "X.")

Only JCL or the operator can set UPSI switches. There's no way
for a program to set UPSI switches or for JCL or the operator to
read them. UPSI provides one-way communication from JCL to
the program.

Check Your Understanding

1. Which statements about the communication region are true?
   a. It is a memory area.
   b. It is a disk file.
   c. All partitions share one communication region.
   d. Each partition has its own communication region.
   e. It is cleared (reset) at the beginning of each job.
   f. It is cleared (reset) at the beginning of each step.
   g. It is cleared (reset) only when the system is IPL'd.

2. The UPSI byte provides . . .
   a. Program-to-program communication.
   b. JCL-to-program communication.
   c. Program-to-operator communication.

3. Suppose a program sorts records in ascending order if UPSI-0 is off, descending order if it's on. Write a JCL statement requesting a descending sort.

✔ **Answers**

1. a, d, e

2. b

3. `// UPSI 1XXXXXXX` or `// UPSI 10000000` or `// UPSI 1`

The PAUSE Statement

The PAUSE statement causes job processing to stop. The PAUSE statement appears on the operator's console. When the operator enters a response, processing resumes. The format of the PAUSE statement is:

```
// PAUSE   any user comment
```

Examples:

```
// PAUSE    five copies of this report, please

// PAUSE    please mount vol 356900 on 281.

// PAUSE    Job time estimated at five hours
```

Use this statement when you want to catch the operator's attention. The operator must respond before the job can continue. Obviously, you should exercise restraint in using it. It lessens system throughput and pulls the operator away from other tasks.

✓ Check Your Understanding

Suppose you're creating a tape to be shipped to another installation. You want a new tape, 2400 feet long, with no volume labels.

Write a JCL statement to tell the operator what you want.

✔ Answer

```
// PAUSE    Output tape should be new, 2400 feet, no volume labels
```

The MTC Statement

For the most part, VSE handles tape volumes automatically. But you can override automatic handling with the MTC statement. This can be useful when preparing tapes for or processing tapes from other systems.

The format of the MTC statement is:

$$// \text{ MTC} \quad \text{operation,} \begin{Bmatrix} \text{SYSxxx} \\ \text{address} \end{Bmatrix} \text{ [,number of times]}$$

The operation specifies what you want done. Here are some of the operations (others are explained in your JCL manual):

WTM Writes a tapemark on the tape. (Tapemarks separate files and labels on tape.)

REW Rewinds the reel.

RUN Rewinds and unloads the reel.

DSE Erases data from the current position to the end of the volume; provides better security for sensitive data than just letting a file get overwritten after it has expired.

SYSxxx or address tells VSE which volume to use. Number of times indicates how many times the operation should be repeated. Here are some examples:

// MTC WTM,SYS030,6	Writes six consecutive tapemarks on logical unit SYS030.
// MTC REW,SYS136	Rewinds logical unit SYS136.
// MTC WTM,SYS030,2 **// MTC DSE,SYS030**	Writes two tapemarks, then erases rest of reel at logical unit SYS030.

✓ Check Your Understanding

1. Write a set of statements to rewind SYS007 to the beginning, erase the entire tape, then rewind and unload the tape.

2. Write a statement to write two tapemarks at the current position on SYS008.

✔ Answers

1. `// MTC REW,SYS007`
   `// MTC DSE,SYS007`
   `// MTC RUN,SYS007`

2. `// MTC WTM,SYS008,2`

The LIBDROP Statement

You've seen how to attach libraries to a partition using LIB-DEF. You can replace that definition simply by submitting another LIBDEF statement. But if you want to cancel libraries without providing others, use LIBDROP:

$$
\text{// LIBDROP} \quad \left\{ \begin{matrix} \text{CL} \\ \text{RL} \\ \text{SL} \\ \text{PL} \end{matrix} \right\} \quad \left\{ \begin{matrix} \text{[SEARCH][,FROM][,TO]} \\ \text{,ALL} \end{matrix} \right\} \quad \left[\begin{matrix} \text{,PERM} \\ \text{,TEMP} \end{matrix} \right]
$$

The codes CL, RL, SL, and PL have the same meaning as in LIBDEF. If you want to cancel all temporary Core Image Libraries, you would code:

```
// LIBDROP    CL,ALL
```

TEMP is the default, so you don't need to code it. The other operands are not needed too often. If you need to drop a specific library or have other special requirements, check out LIBDROP in your manual.

✓ Check Your Understanding

For step 1 of a job, you defined a temporary source statement search chain. However, step 2 will run faster if the permanent chain is used. Write a statement to cancel the temporary chain.

✔ Answer

```
// LIBDROP    SL,SEARCH
```

LIBLIST and LISTIO

Sometimes you may need to find out what the various library and I/O assignments are and no one is available to get the information for you. LIBLIST lists the library assignments and LISTIO lists I/O assignments. Here's LIBLIST:

$$
// \text{ LIBLIST } \begin{Bmatrix} CL \\ RL \\ SL \\ PL \end{Bmatrix} \begin{bmatrix} , BG \\ , Fn \\ , * \\ , ALL \end{bmatrix}
$$

You specify which type of library and which partition you're interested in. (* means the current partition and is the default.) For example, suppose you want to find out the Procedure Library definitions for the current partition:

`// LIBLIST     PL`   or   `// LIBLIST     PL,*`

To get a list of all the Core Image Library definitions, you'd use:

`// LIBLIST     CL,ALL`

The LISTIO statement can tell you what I/O units are currently assigned. Here's the format:

$$
// \text{ LISTIO } \begin{Bmatrix} ASSGN \\ PROG \\ SYS \\ SYSxxx \\ BG \\ Fn \\ "address" \\ ALL \\ UNITS \\ DOWN \\ UA \end{Bmatrix}
$$

Each option gives you slightly different information. ASSGN asks for all the units assigned to the partition issuing the LISTIO statement, the current partition. PROG asks for all the programmer logical units (such as SYS007) assigned to the current partition while SYS asks for all the system logical units (such as SYSRDR). SYSxxx requests the physical unit or units assigned to the indicated logical unit for the current partition.

BG or Fn requests all the units assigned to the indicated background or foreground partition.

"Address" lists all the logical units assigned to the addressed physical unit across all partitions. ALL lists all the physical units assigned to each logical unit across all partitions, while UNITS does the reverse, listing all logical units assigned to each physical unit.

DOWN lists all the physical units that are currently inoperative and UA lists all the physical units not currently assigned to logical units.

Most of these items are probably more useful to the operator and system programmers than to you. However, you may find these statements handy:

```
// LISTIO    ASSGN

// LISTIO    BG

// LISTIO    F1          (or whatever)

// LISTIO    ALL
```

Include the LISTIO statement in any job.

✓ Check Your Understanding

1. Write a statement to find out all the Core Image Library assignments for whatever partition you're using.

2. Write a statement to find out all the Source Statement Library assignments for the F4 partition.

3. Write a statement to find out all the logical units assigned to the partition you're using.

4. Write a statement to find out all the physical units assigned to each logical unit at your installation, regardless of partition.

✔ Answers

1. `// LIBLIST    CL`   or `// LIBLIST    CL,*`

2. `// LIBLIST    SL,F4`

3. `// LISTIO     ASSGN`

4. `// LISTIO     ALL`

The SETPRT Statement

If your installation has an IBM 3800 Printing Subsystem, you have a lot of control over how your jobs are printed. The SETPRT statement gives you that control. You can specify such things as whether the report should be automatically burst and trimmed, what print fonts to use, and what form (paper) to use.

The format of SETPRT is:

```
//SETPRT    SYSxxx,characteristic[,characteristic...]
```

SYSxxx identifies the report you're controlling, usually SYSLST. But if a program involves more than one printout (for example, SYSLST, SYS005, and SYS006) and you have different specifications for each one, your job may look something like this:

```
// JOB    REPORTER
// ASSGN  SYS005,SYSLST
// ASSGN  SYS006,SYSLST
// SETPRT SYSLST,(characteristics of first report)
// SETPRT SYS005,(characteristics of second report)
// SETPRT SYS006,(characteristics of third report)
...
```

Now all three logical units are assigned to the same physical unit (we're assuming here that SYSLST is permanently assigned to the 3800PS). The three SETPRT statements set up the print characteristics of the three reports.

Now let's look at the characteristics you can specify. We'll briefly discuss some common ones. If you want more details, see your 3800PS manuals.

BURST= refers to the burster-trimmer-stacker device, which removes margins and separates pages. If you want the operator to feed the report into the burster-trimmer-stacker, specify BURST = Y. If not, specify BURST = N. If you want to go with the system default, specify BURST = *. If you don't care, omit the operand and no change will take place, thus causing the least amount of operator involvement and taking the least amount of time.

Several operands help you format the page. CHARS = selects from one to four character sets (fonts). Get the names of your installation's character sets from a friendly local expert. If you specify only one name, the entire report is printed in that print style. If you specify more than one, the print records should include special characters indicating where to use which font (1, 2, 3, or 4); your application program must place the font selection characters in the print records. To specify one character set, use this format: CHARS = FM10. To specify more than one: CHARS = (FM10,FM12,IT10). To request the default: CHARS = *. To go with the current character set, whatever it is, leave out the CHARS = operand.

FCB= selects a forms control buffer, which formats the printed page. The FCB includes such things as page length, margins, and number of lines per inch. Your installation will have several FCBs stored online. You'll need to find out their names and how to define your own if necessary. FCB = STD1 selects the FCB named STD1. FCB = * selects the default FCB. Omitting the operand continues whatever FCB is currently in use.

If you're changing the FCB, you might want to verify that the format you've selected fits properly with your paper. The V operand asks the system to print a verification page using sample data. Then you or the operator can check the sample page before printing the job. To do this, specify FCB = (fcbname,V) or FCB = (*,V).

FORMS= specifies the paper to be used. You'll need to find out the names of the forms available at your installation. FORMS = GB11 selects the form named GB11, while FORMS = * requests the default form. VSE asks the operator to load the requested form. If you don't care, omit the FORMS = operand and the operator won't get involved. If you change forms from the standard, you'll probably need to change the FCB to match the form you've selected.

Use FLASH= if you want to overprint artwork such as logos and boxes on your pages. The artwork is copied from a specially prepared overlay form by a xerographic process at the same time the data records are formatted and printed. The operator installs the requested overlay on the machine. It's the program's responsibility to make the data records fit with the artwork on the page. FLASH=LOGO asks for the overlay named LOGO to be printed on every page, while FLASH=* asks for the default overlay (probably none). FLASH=(LOGO,2) asks for the form named LOGO to be copied on the first two pages only.

Figure 9.1 summarizes the operands discussed here. There are several other SETPRT operands you can use in certain situations, but these are the most common. If your installation has a 3800PS, spend some time getting to know its features and how you can use them. Your clients will appreciate it.

Figure 9.1 Selected SETPRT Operands

BURST	Trim and separate pages
CHARS	Select character set(s)
FCB	Format printed page
FORMS	Paper type
FLASH	Overprint graphics

 Check Your Understanding

1. Write a statement for SYSLST that selects the form named 8X10, the FCB named GF10, and the character set named AB12. Verify the FCB before using it.

2. Write a statement for SYSLST that selects the default form, the default FCB, and the default character set. Ask for overlay form BOX1. Burst, trim, and stack the report.

✔ Answers

1. `// SETPRT    SYSLST,FORMS=8X10,FCB=(GF10,V)CHARS=AB12`

2. `// SETPRT    SYSLST,FORMS=*,FCB=*,CHARS=*,FLASH=BOX1,BURST=Y`

The ASSGN Statement

You've seen the most useful parameters of the ASSGN statement, but you should be aware of three more: UA, IGN, and
ALT.

Here's an expanded format of the ASSGN statement showing
these additional three parameters:

```
                    ( address        )
                    | address-list   |
                    | symbolic-unit  |                  [,TEMP] [,SHR]
// ASSGN symbolic-unit, | class     |  [,VOL=number] [,PERM] [,ALT]
                    | type           |
                    | UA             |
                    ( IGN            )
```

UA says to unassign a unit; it undoes a previous assignment and
leaves the unit with no assignment. IGN says to ignore a unit;
you might want to do this during debugging when you don't
want to provide an input file or produce an output file. When a
unit is ignored, VSE simply ignores all I/O commands for that
file. ALT is used only with multivolume tape files. It provides an
alternate drive that can be readied by the operator while the
original drive is in use. Then when the first volume is finished,
VSE automatically switches to the next volume on the alternate drive. Now the operator can remove the first volume from
the original drive and mount the third volume there. Thus, the
job doesn't have to wait while tape reels are exchanged. Here's
an example of an assignment for a multivolume output file:

```
// ASSGN SYS008,2400
// ASSGN SYS008,2400,ALT
```

Check Your Understanding

1. Write a statement that causes all references to SYS008 to be ignored during this job.

2. Write a statement that unassigns SYS050.

3. Write two statements to set up tape drives 181 and 182 as alternates for the file on SYS009.

✔ Answers

1. `// ASSGN SYS008,IGN`

2. `// ASSGN SYS050,UA`

3. `// ASSGN SYS009,181`
   `// ASSGN SYS009,182,ALT`

The EXEC Statement

Here's an expanded format for the EXEC statement showing a parameter we have not discussed before:

```
// EXEC  [ [PGM=]phasename[,REAL][SIZE=size][,GO] ]
        [ PROC=procname[,OV]                       ]
```

The REAL operand forces VSE to keep the entire program within real memory; no part of the program is ever paged out. "Ah hah," you say, "I can make my programs run much faster this way." "Oh no," say your fellow users, "you'll make our programs run much slower if you do." Your installation probably bans the REAL operand without special dispensation from the boss.

By the way, if you use more than one optional EXEC operand, they must be in the order shown, even though they're keyword operands. You don't have to code commas for missing operands, however. For example, this is *not* correct:

```
EXEC LASTSTAR,SIZE=AUTO,REAL
```

It should be:

```
EXEC LASTSTAR,REAL,SIZE=AUTO
```

⟋ Check Your Understanding

1. True or false? REAL makes your programs run faster and you should put it on every EXEC statement.

2. What's wrong with this statement:

```
// EXEC FCOBOL,GO,SIZE=AUTO
```

✔ Answers

1. False. It should be avoided because it makes your programs run faster at the expense of the programs in the other partitions.

2. Two major things are wrong:
    a. GO and SIZE= are out of order.
    b. SIZE=AUTO should not be used with compilers and linkage editors.

Chapter Summary

This chapter has briefly touched on a number of items you should be aware of, even if you don't use them too often. DATE changes the system date for this job only. UPSI sets switches that can be tested by the program. PAUSE halts the job until the system operator responds to a message. MTC controls processing of tape reels. LIBDROP eliminates a library definition. LIBLIST lists library definitions. LISTIO lists I/O assignments. SETPRT controls printing on the 3800PS. The ASSGN statement can be used to unassign (UA) or ignore (IGN) a unit and to establish alternate tape drives (ALT). You can force a program to run in real memory with the REAL operand of the EXEC statement, but you probably shouldn't.

✓ Chapter Exercise

1. Match.

    _____ a. UPSI   A. Controls tape handling
    _____ b. PAUSE   B. Passes data to program
    _____ c. MTC   C. Clears (zeros) memory
    _____ d. SETPRT   D. Controls the 3800PS
                                     E. Communicates with the operator

2. Match.

    _____ a. LIBDROP   A. Cancels unit assignments
    _____ b. LIBLIST   B. Cancels library assignments
    _____ c. LISTIO   C. Lists unit assignments
                                       D. Lists library assignments

3. Match.

    _____ a. UA   A. Establishes alternate tape drives
    _____ b. IGN
    _____ c. ALT   B. Establishes alternate disk drives
                                       C. Causes I/O statements to not be executed
                                       D. Causes a unit to have no assignment

4. Select the true statements.
   a. REAL forces a program to be stored entirely in real memory.
   b. REAL makes a program execute faster.
   c. Most programmers use REAL with every program.

5. Write statements to accomplish the following functions:
   a. Set the system date to March 17, 1990, American style.
   b. Turn on the first UPSI switch, turn off the second, and leave the others alone.
   c. Force the job to stop until the operator signals that private volume 149001 has been removed and write protected.
   d. Write two tapemarks on SYS004.
   e. Remove all temporary Core Image Library assignments.
   f. List all the physical unit assignments for all the partitions.
   g. List all the Source Statement Library assignments for the current partition.
   h. Cause SYS010 to have no assignment.
   i. Cause VSE to ignore all I/O requests for SYS011.
   j. Set up two alternate tape units (3400) for SYS012.
   k. Force the program named FASTRACK to be run in real memory.

✔ **Answers to Chapter Exercise**

1. a - B; b - E; c - A; d - D

2. a - B; b - D; c - C

3. a - D; b - C; c - A

4. a, b

5. a. `// DATE 3/17/90`

   b. `// UPSI 10 or // UPSI 10xxxxxx`

   c. `// PAUSE PLEASE REMOVE VOLUME 149001 AND WRITE PROTECT`

   d. `// MTC WTM,SYS004,2`

   e. `// LIBDROP CL,ALL`

f. `// LISTIO ALL`

g. `// LIBLIST SL,*`

h. `// ASSGN SYS010,UA`

i. `// ASSGN SYS011,IGN`

j. `// ASSGN SYS012,3400`
   `// ASSGN SYS012,3400,ALT`

k. `// EXEC FASTRACK,REAL`

Summary of JCL Options

	Tape	CKD
		SAM

	Tape	CKD
Input files	**[ASSGN]** symbolic-unit physical-unit [TEMP/PERM] VOL= [ALT] **TLBL** filename ['file-ID'] [date] [file-serial-number] [volume-sequence-number] [file-sequence-number] [generation-number] [version-number]	**[ASSGN]** symbolic-unit physical-unit [TEMP/PERM] VOL= [SHR] **DLBL** filename ['file-ID'] [code] [BLKSIZE=] **[EXTENT]*** [symbolic-unit] [volume-serial-number]
Output files	**[ASSGN]** symbolic-unit physical-unit [TEMP/PERM] [VOL=] [ALT] **TLBL** filename ['file-ID'] [date] [file-serial-number] [volume-sequence-number] [file-sequence-number] [generation-number] [version-number]	**[ASSGN]** symbolic-unit physical-unit [TEMP/PERM] [VOL=] [SHR] **DLBL** filename ['file-ID'] [date] [code] [DSF] [BLKSIZE=] **EXTENT** [symbolic-unit] [volume-serial-number] [type] [sequence-number] [starting-track] [number-of-tracks]

* Use only when multiple input volumes are involved

for Various Types of Files

	SAM		VSAM
FBA	**Diskette**		**VSAM**

FBA	Diskette	VSAM
[ASSGN] symbolic-unit physical-unit [TEMP/PERM] VOL = [SHR]	**[ASSGN]** symbolic-unit physical-unit [TEMP/PERM] VOL =	**[ASSGN]** symbolic-unit physical-unit [TEMP/PERM]
DLBL filename ['file-ID'] [code] [CISIZE =]	**DLBL** filename ['file-ID'] DU	**DLBL** filename ['file-ID'] VSAM [CAT =]
[EXTENT]* [symbolic-unit] [volume-serial-number]	**[EXTENT]*** [symbolic-unit] [volume-serial-number]	
[ASSGN] symbolic-unit physical-unit [TEMP/PERM] [VOL =] [SHR]	**[ASSGN]** symbolic-unit physical-unit [TEMP/PERM] [VOL =]	**[ASSGN]** symbolic-unit physical-unit [TEMP/PERM]
DLBL filename ['file-ID'] [date] [code] [DSF] [CISIZE =]	**DLBL** filename ['file-ID'] [date] Du	**DLBL** filename ['file-ID'] [date] VSAM [CAT =]
EXTENT [symbolic-unit] [volume-serial-number] [type] [sequence-number] [starting-block] [number-of-blocks]	**EXTENT** [symbolic-unit] [volume-serial-number]	

Index